IT'S ALL DONE WITH NUMBERS

Easy to Learn, Easy to Do

Mind-reading Tricks

Lightning Calculations

Uncanny Predictions

Spooky Illusions

Mad Math Routines

Fortunetelling Fakery

**For Young and Old
Amateurs and Professionals,
Ladies and Gentlemen**

**Doubleday & Company, Inc.
Garden City, New York**

IT'S ALL DONE WITH NUMBERS

Astounding and Confounding Feats of Mathematical Magic

Rose Wyler and
Gerald Ames

Illustrated by Carter Jones

Rose Wyler, who is well known for her many science and science-puzzle books, is also known to many as the coauthor of numerous magic books with her husband, Gerald Ames. She has taught elementary science in New York public schools and science education at Columbia and has also done field work in astronomy, biology, and geology. Gerald Ames, an accomplished artist, also has a long list of books for young readers to his credit. They live and work in New York City and spend their summers in Maine.

Library of Congress Cataloging in Publication Data

Wyler, Rose.
   It's all done with numbers.

   Includes index.
   SUMMARY: Presents step-by-step instructions for mind reading and prediction tricks based on elementary mathematics.
   1. Mathematical recreations—Juvenile literature.   [1. Mathematical recreations.   2. Magic tricks]   I. Ames, Gerald.   II. Jones, Carter.
II.   Title.
QA95.W944   793.7'4
ISBN: 0-385-03059-2 Trade
ISBN: 0-385-09003-X Prebound
Library of Congress Catalog Card Number 76–42416

CONTENTS

1. THE MAGIC OF 1, 2, 3 . . .

Out of the magician's hat comes the rabbit, into nowhere go the coins, from unlikely places appear eggs, pigeons, even an elephant. In contriving these illusions, the magician depends on sleight of hand, special boxes and other props, and skillful misdirection by which he persuades you to see just what he wants you to see.

Tricks that fool the eye are amazing enough, but a trick that fools the mind can produce a far greater sense of bafflement and mystery. As a rule, no props are used, and this in itself contributes to the uncanny effect. The performer convinces you that he can do the impossible with the power of his mind alone.

Impressive as it is, mental magic is not hard to do. The tricks require no manual skill. Many are based on math—but easy math that just seems hard. It is such tricks—simple yet effective—that we present in this book.

Professor Thinkfast's Mind-reading Trick

A hostess, announcing that the evening's entertainment will be some mental magic, introduces the performer as the "famous Professor Thinkfast." Okay, the guests say to themselves, but can this Professor really do good magic without a high hat, a wand, a cape, and other props?

They soon find that he can, for he has something better than props: a good presentation.

Professor Thinkfast calls for a volunteer, and from among the several people who respond, he chooses a young woman named Susan.

"Please," the Professor says to Susan, "prepare to write down four numbers, which you will add. First, the year of your birth.

Susan writes.

"I believe I am receiving the number in thought waves," says the Professor. "Next, the year of a very important event in your life."

Susan writes.

"Next, the age you will be at the end of the present year. And finally, the number of years that have passed since the important event."

As Susan begins to add, Professor Thinkfast quickly writes down a number. When Susan compares his total with hers, it is the same: 3958.

How does the Professor do it? Simply by multiplying the current year, which is 1979, by 2.

Why does the trick work? Two of the numbers, the year of Susan's birth and her age at the end of the year, add up to 1979. And if the big event was Susan's marriage, in 1975, that year, plus the 4 years since, also gives 1979.

Math in Disguise

The Professor's trick is, of course, a math trick thinly disguised as mind reading. This pretense is in keeping with tradition.

In the days of vaudeville, magicians played down the math in their acts. Perhaps they thought the very word would scare people away. Worse still, they feared that calling attention to the math might spoil the magical effect.

Dunninger, the great mind reader, covered up his math so well that audiences never realized some of his most sensational feats were really number tricks—and fairly simple ones at that. When card experts, fortunetellers, mediums, and seers used math in their shows, they, too, disguised it as much as possible. Only one kind of entertainer openly featured math. This was the calculating wizard, who pretended to solve difficult problems in his head, at lightning speed.

Performing Tricks That Fool the Mind

Pocket calculators have brought about a new cycle of interest in number tricks. Although most of the tricks can be performed without a calculator, the instrument assures accuracy and speeds up checking the results. Its use has made mathematical magic more popular than ever among professionals, and also among amateurs, for whom it is well suited.

Mathematical magic can be performed almost anywhere. Props are unnecessary, since the tricks deal with numbers, not things. When coins, dice, cards, or dominoes are used, they just stand for numbers. The tricks do not call for sleight of hand or even any special mathematical talent. If you can add and subtract, multiply and divide, you can understand the tricks in this book, and you can perform them, too. In fact, you can put on a good show without understanding why most of the tricks work.

When explanations are needed for preparing a trick, they are included with the stage directions. Otherwise they are given in Chapter 8, called "Aftermath."

For a smooth performance, you will do well to rehearse the patter that goes with a trick. It is important for building up interest and for directing or *misdirecting* the audience's attention. Samples of patter are given with the tricks that follow. Use them if they appeal to you, or develop versions of your own. In any case, don't try to memorize patter. Just have a general outline in mind; then your delivery can be easygoing and natural. You can keep your eye on the audience, and speed up or slow down according to how they react.

After you have practiced a few tricks by yourself or with a friend or two, you may venture putting on a short act before a group. As a performer, you have a choice of rules. You may decide to be a mind reader, a lightning calculator, a fortune-teller, a medium familiar with spooks, a cardsharp, or a stand-up comic.

In each of the following chapters, a different role is featured along with tricks suitable to the role. This arrangement will help you in planning a program. The important thing is to choose a role and stick to it. Then the act will hang together, and each trick will seem better than the one before. Jumping from one role to another would spoil the effect. If you *must* try various roles—and why not?—do so on different occasions.

Lady Magicians, Attention!

As we know, it is always a lady who is sawed in half—and by a male magician. The Great and Famous So-and-so is practically always a man. If a girl is on stage with him, she must act the "dumb but pretty" girl who, at the right moment, draws attention away from the mechanics of a trick. "Look at her," the old-fashioned magician says; "she can't add, but she sure can distract."

Boo-o-o-o!

It's time—isn't it?—that there were some girl performers. Mental magic offers roles in which a woman can do as well as a man, perhaps better. So, instead of ladies being sawed in half, let's have lady magicians.

Puzzlers for Puzzle Fans

For anybody, male or female, number magic has a special advantage. Unlike the fool-the-eye magic, it can be enjoyed by one person alone. Someone who has no interest in performing can take up the tricks as entertaining puzzles.

A number trick often hinges on some well-concealed principle. Can you penetrate this inner secret? If you are a puzzle fan, you accept the challenge and will try to work out the puzzles that follow several of the tricks. Answers are given at the end of the book, on pages you are referred to in "Aftermath."

No doubt you will want to try some favorite teasers on friends. For a real baffler, do the trick first, then spring the problem: why does it work? You will find that a combination of trick and tease is entertaining even to people who think they hate puzzles.

Of course, when performing the tricks as magic, you must not reveal how they are done and why they work. That would spoil the atmosphere of mystery.

However you decide to use the tricks, whether as brain teasers or as magic, have fun! Amaze yourself as well as your friends. Welcome, all of you, to the world of the mental magicians, the mysterious world where it's all done with numbers.

2. TRICKS THE MIND READER KEEPS IN MIND

Pick Any Number
Pick Any Card
Dunninger's Brain Buster
Psychic Pet
Blind Man's Bluff
Telephoney
ESP for Colors
Heads or Tails?
Mental Television

Mind-reading acts have mystified audiences ever since the golden age of vaudeville. In those days, when a few thousand magicians were touring the country, most of them performed as mind readers at one time or another. Borrowing and improving on one another's ideas, they developed tricks that were masterpieces of deception.

Publicity for their acts was as good as the tricks. Sometimes a performer would appear in town with a horse and buggy and drive, blindfolded, through the streets. Supposedly, he found his way by a mysterious faculty called second sight, though actually he just peeked through small holes in the blindfold.

At show time, the performer gave further demonstrations of second sight. Often he would sit blindfolded on stage while an assistant went through the audience touching objects that people would offer. Could the performer name the objects? Always! In its simplest form, the trick depended on a code of ten words used by the assistant. Each word stood for one of the ten digits, and two words would be combined for a two-digit number. For example, if "tell" stood for 1 and "answer" for 2, "Tell me the answer" meant 12; and 12 stood for one item on a numbered list of articles—keys, coins, a watch, etc.—that people might show to the assistant.

In a typical act, the performer would prove his mind-reading powers by going through various tests. A volunteer would concentrate on a chosen playing card, and the performer would name it. Or the volunteer would pick a particular time of day, and the performer would give the hour and minute he was thinking of.

The mind reader sometimes relied on a confederate, but not always. Some tricks were done with a prepared deck of cards; some were rigged to work automatically; others depended on suggestion to steer a spectator toward the desired answer.

All these methods of deception are still in use. Only the patter is a little different. Nowadays, performers like to talk about "extrasensory perception"—ESP for short. Instead of second sight, they speak of clairvoyance; instead of mind reading, they say telepathy.

Though patter has changed, the old rules for fooling people still hold. For example, if you perform as a mind reader, you must be serious in manner. Then the audience will take you seriously. Jokes and nonsense would spoil the impressiveness of your act. Another important thing to remember is that an audience gets weary if the session is too long. Three or four tricks are enough—five at the most. Dunninger, great showman that he was, never tried to hold an audience for more than half an hour.

If a trick doesn't come out right, don't panic. Just say you are under a strain, for mind reading is hard work. No one expects you to be right 100 per cent of the time. In fact, a few mistakes will make your effort seem genuine.

Pick Any Number

This trick, good as an opener, is a test of your mind-reading power. Who will give you the test? Let's say that Tony volunteers.

"Pick a number that's easy to remember," you tell him. "Pick one that's less than 50 and that has two digits—two odd digits that are not the same." You look directly at Tony, write 37 on a card, and say, "You are skipping numbers like 11, in which both digits are the same. Right? I seem to be able to follow your thought waves. Well, tell us your number and let's see if it's the one I have written down."

Will Tony's number be 37? Probably.

And if not, it is likely to be 35 or 39. In that case, you can remark that you did come close. Perhaps static kept you from getting perfect reception.

The same excuse can be used in the unlikely event that you were even farther off. Actually, the volunteer's choice is quite limited. Only eight numbers under 50 contain two different odd digits: 13, 15, 17, 19, 31, 35, 37, and 39. And you try to narrow the choice still more by mentioning the number 11 as unacceptable. This tends to turn the volunteer's thoughts away from numbers that begin or end with 1; then only three numbers are left to choose from: 35, 37, and 39. Of the three, more often than not, the volunteer picks 37. Why? Perhaps because there is a 7 in it, and 7 is a favorite number of many people.

If the audience followed Tony in "picking a number," it is likely that many of them also chose 37. But the less said about this, the better. People might realize that you practically forced Tony's choice. So, quick! on to another trick.

Pick Any Card

Before Houdini became famous for his escape act, he and his wife, Beatrice, were mind readers in circus side shows. This was one of their tricks. In writing about it, Houdini said that although any team could do the trick after a little practice, it made "baffling entertainment," particularly if it was "used before a small and discriminating audience."

The trick is still a puzzler. You and a friend can present it as a mind-reading demonstration, and no one will figure out how you do it.

As far as the audience can tell, this is what happens: Your partner, seated at a table, displays a deck of cards. While your back is turned, someone chooses a card and shows it to the rest of the audience. Your partner returns it to the deck and puts the deck on the table. When you turn around, you and your partner stare at one another, concentrating intently. Can you name the chosen card? Naturally, you do.

The demonstration can be repeated without giving away the secret, for in the code you use, the signals are silent. It all depends on how your partner places the deck on the table.

In practicing the trick, draw a large rectangle on the table top, and divide it into a grid with twelve places, as in the diagram. Then you and your partner practice putting the deck where it should go. If the chosen card is an ace, the deck goes into space 1. If it is a card from 2 to 10, the deck goes into the proper space. Spaces 11 and 12 are for the jack and the queen. The position for the king is outside the grid.

Through practice, you and your partner fix the grid in your minds. Then, when performing, you have a clear mental picture of it. To make things easier, you could use a desk blotter or something of that shape for your rectangle.

The location of the deck on the imaginary grid tells which numbered or face card has been chosen. The suit is indicated by the position of the deck with respect to the mind reader. As shown in the diagram, it is placed horizontally for hearts, vertically for clubs, or angled to the left or right for spades or diamonds.

Dunninger's Brain Buster

Dunninger called this trick a brain buster because he thought it was one of his best. Sometimes he performed it as a magic card trick, and sometimes he made it look like an experiment in extrasensory perception.

Dunninger wrote that on one occasion he did the trick for Thomas Edison and three of his friends. The inventor had been talking about mental telepathy and mentioned instances when the same thought had occurred to him and his co-workers at the same time. This led to an interesting question. Could a group of people bring about a planned result if all of them concentrated on it?

Dunninger said he knew of an experiment to test this possibility. It was an attempt, by combined mental effort, to bring a buried card to the top of the deck. Naturally, Edison and his friends wanted to do the "experiment," and naturally, Dunninger had a deck of cards with him. He handed the deck to Edison and, turning his back to the group, began telling them what to do.

This is what happened:

1. Edison counted off a number of cards—fewer than twelve—and put them in his pocket. (Let's assume he pocketed five cards.)

2. He counted off the same number again and looked at the card at the bottom of the packet. This was the card to be buried. (Assume it was the ace of hearts.) Then he put the packet back on top of the deck.

3. At this point Edison's three friends joined the "experiment." Each thought of a person's name; then each in turn took the pack and dealt out cards, one for each letter of the name he had in mind. (We'll assume the names were Jane, Dick, and Tom.)

4. Each man, in turn, put the cards he had counted off back on the pack.

5. Edison put the five cards from his pocket on top of the pack.

6. Now to bring the buried card to the top. Only Edison knew what it was; the others were told to try to reinforce his mental effort. Each in turn again counted off cards for the name he had chosen.

When the third friend had finished, Dunninger asked Edison to name his card.

"The ace of hearts," said Edison.

"If that card is now on top," Dunninger remarked, "we might say some form of thought power got it there. Would you turn over the top card?"

Edison did, and it was the ace of hearts.

Edison and his friends were so impressed with the result, they found it hard to believe the "experiment" was a fake. To convince them, Dunninger asked them to analyze the trick. They tried but gave up and had to have it explained.

Actually, the trick is fairly simple. It works automatically, as you can see if you take a deck and go through the steps with the buried card face up.

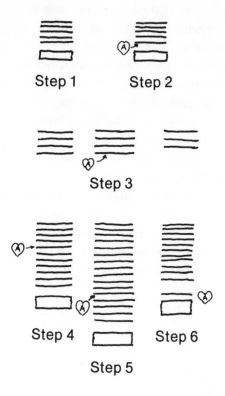

Step 1   Step 2

Step 3

Step 4   Step 6

Step 5

This diagram shows what happens. As a result of steps 3 and 4 (counting off cards for the names and then returning them), eleven cards at the top of the deck are reversed. This shifts the ace of hearts from its original, fifth position to seventh. When the five pocketed cards are added, in step 5, The ace of hearts is placed in twelfth position. Then, when eleven cards are again counted off for the names, in step 6, the ace of hearts is at the top of the pack.

The spelling out of names confuses people. They do not realize that after piling a certain numbers of cards on the buried card, they take away the same number. The math of the trick is simple—just adding and subtracting. But Thomas Edison couldn't figure it out!

Psychic Pet

A number of magicians owning pets have trained them to be performers. Houdini, the escape artist, had a dog, named Bobby, that learned to escape from almost any restraint. Bobby could get out of entangling ropes and from little handcuffs that were made especially for him. The Handcuff King of Dogs, Houdini called him.

Mind readers, it seems, have preferred to train cats. One magician, who performed in England, would pretend to send thought waves to his cat, telling it to do such things as lick its left paw or scratch its right ear. And the cat, apparently getting the message, did what was required. The magician had made sure of the cat's co-operation by secretly rubbing its paw or ear with a dab of butter. In another trick, the cat would be induced to go to a certain corner—for a bit of catnip hidden there.

If you have a cat, why not get it to perform? While the cat is kept in the next room and cannot see what is going on, ask someone to choose a card for it to identify. You then scatter the cards around, placing the chosen card near some hidden catnip. When the cat is brought in, hold it and pretend you are concentrating on the selected card. Then release your psychic pet and . . . well, you know what will happen.

Blind Man's Bluff

For this trick, an assistant blindfolds you, then describes the feat you will perform. Several problems will be made up by the audience, and you, without hearing or seeing a single number, will get each answer from people's thought waves.

The assistant calls three persons to the blackboard. (You keep your back toward it.) The first person writes down a single digit. The second puts a smaller digit under it. The third completes the problem with a plus or a minus or a multiplication sign.

Suppose this is what they write:

$$8$$
$$-3$$

The assistant tells the audience to concentrate on the problem, then asks you, "Can you pick up their thoughts and tell us the answer?"

Hesitating a little, you say, "Five."

Two or three times more, a problem is silently put down behind your back; and each time, you get the answer.

Most of the audience will realize that your assistant signals the answers, but they don't know how. Here is the code:

Oh 0   For a one-digit answer, the assistant gives the
I 1   code word for the number, then says, "Tell us
So 2   the answer." But he starts with that phrase
There 3   when the answer has two digits, then adds a
For 4   phrase with the code words for each digit. To
And 5   signal 5, he just says, "And tell us the answer."
And I 6   But, to signal 51, he might say, "Tell us the
And so 7   answer and speak loud. I want to hear it."
And there 8
And for 9

Simple enough, but rehearsals are necessary before you can do the trick smoothly.

Telephoney

In this trick, you propose to mind-read a number with several digits—in fact, a phone number. A volunteer from the audience will pick the number from the telephone book, and you will try to receive his or her thought waves and get the number.

When John volunteers, you hand him three dice. The dice, you explain, will be used in selecting a page in the directory. Then, no one can think that you and John agreed on a number in advance.

While your back is turned, John rolls the dice until he gets three different numbers. He writes them down in any order he wishes, to form a three-digit number. Then he *reverses* the digits and subtracts the smaller of the two numbers from the larger. Say these are John's figures:

$$543$$
$$-345$$
$$\overline{198}$$

Using the result, John turns to page 198 of the directory, notes the first phone number listed, and concentrates on it.

Meanwhile, you, too, are concentrating. "I seem to be getting the last digit first—a 7, but I may be wrong. Am I, John?"

If John says you are wrong, you try again. When you get it right, you go on to the next-to-the-last digit and to the others, which you get without checking with John. Finally, you have a complete phone number. Is it the one listed first on the selected page? Yes, it is.

How do you work the trick?

By limiting the volunteer's choices. The dice help, since they give no digit higher than 6. This rules out any three-digit number above 654. And there are only five possible results of the subtraction: 99, 198, 297, 396, and 495.

If your directory has fewer than 495 pages, tell the volunteer to take the result and divide it by 9. This will give: 11, 22, 33, 44, or 55.

In either case, the page selected will be one of five possibilities, and the phone number, too, will be one of five. You look up the numbers in advance and write them on the palm of your hand or on a slip of paper that you glance at secretly.

To get the right number, you fish around until you have the last digit, or the last two; then you can give the whole number.

FOR PUZZLE FANS

The trick is telephoney, but the math is straight. Try the arithmetic with several three-digit numbers each of which begins and ends with different digits. Reverse the number and subtract the smaller from the larger one. You might expect to get many different results, but only a few are possible, and these come up again and again. The result is either 99 or a three-digit number divisible by 99. For example:

$$198 \div 99 = 2$$
$$297 \div 99 = 3$$
$$396 \div 99 = 4$$

Can you explain this? If not, see page 126 in the "Aftermath" chapter.

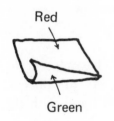

Red

Green

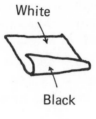

White

Black

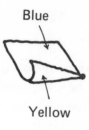

Blue

Yellow

ESP for Colors

This trick may be presented as a demonstration of ESP. You claim it will prove that you can distinguish colors without seeing them.

Three small cards are colored with crayon. One card is red on one side, green on the other; one is white on one side, black on the other; the third is blue on one side, yellow on the other.

A friend—Lucy, let's say—agrees to test you. She is seated at a table with the three cards spread out before her. It doesn't matter which colors lie face up. You look at them, then face the other way. Lucy begins turning over the cards, one at a time. She turns over as many as she wishes, any number of times. Each time she does so, she says, "Turn." When she decides to stop, she covers one card with her hand. Then you turn around and try to figure out which color of the hidden card is face up.

Since you have a fifty-fifty chance of being right just by guessing, there must be several tests. You take them and, each time, you name the color correctly.

How do you do it? With numbers. In your mind, you give a value of 1 to the colors red, white, and blue. To the colors green, black, and yellow, you give a value of zero. Before a test, you mentally add the values of the three colors showing. The smallest possible sum is zero; the highest is 3. You note whether the sum is odd or even (zero is counted as even). Now, when any card is turned over, either 1 is added to the sum or 1 is subtracted. This changes an even sum to odd or an odd sum to even. You keep this in mind as the turning of cards begins.

Suppose a test starts with the three cards lying this way:

You add their values:
red   white   blue
1 + 1 + 1

You say to yourself, "Odd." And when you have faced the other way and hear Lucy say, "Turn," you say to yourself, "Even." With the next "Turn," you say, "Odd"; and with the next, "Even."

At this point, Lucy stops and says you can look, which you do. You know that the sum of the three colors facing up must be even. The two colors that show are, let's say, green (O) and white (1). The blue/yellow card is under Lucy's hand. To make an even sum, blue (1) must be up (0+1+1=2). So you announce, "The color is blue."

Heads or Tails?

In this phony ESP demonstration, coins are tossed while you and several others try to guess the results. The tossing is done far enough away so that none of you can see the coins.

Mary, who gives the tests, explains the first one. Two pennies will be tossed—not together, but one after the other. For each toss there are four possible outcomes:

head, head   (HH)
head, tail   (HT)
tail, head   (TH)
tail, tail   (TT)

The chances of guessing right are one out of four.

The tests start. Four times, the pennies are tossed. While Mary records the results, the rest of you record your guesses.

A score of one out of four is considered average. Four out of four would be extraordinary. Does anybody score four? You do. When the series is repeated, you score three, making one error for the sake of appearances.

Mary then starts another series, in which three coins are tossed, one after another. There are eight possible outcomes:

HHH   THH
HHT   THT
HTH   TTH
HTT   TTT

The three-coin toss is done eight times, and records are kept as before. By guesswork, you might be expected to score one out of eight. But you score seven, claiming you are helped by ESP.

ESP? Of course not. Your secret is a code. Mary is your confederate. She signals the results of tosses with her fingers, showing you any number from zero to seven.

The code involves the binary system of numbers, which is used in computers. These numbers are formed from just two digits: 0 and 1. Letting 0 stand for heads and 1 for tails, you can get binary numbers that describe all the ways the coins land. Here is the key to the code:

Two-coin Toss

coins	binary	signal
HH	00	0
HT	01	1
TH	10	2
TT	11	3

Three-coin Toss

coins	binary	signal
HHH	000	0
HHT	001	1
HTH	010	2
HTT	011	3
THH	100	4
THT	101	5
TTH	110	6
TTT	111	7

When Mary tosses a TH, for example, she codes it into 1 and zero — 10 — and since this is binary for 2, she flashes you a two-finger signal. You translate 2 into binary — — 10 — telling you the toss came out TH.

Later, Mary signals the appropriate number for a three-digit sequence. Again you translate it into binary. This enables you to call the toss and show off your ESP.

Mental Television

This kind of mind-reading trick has a long history. A version of it was performed in Europe two centuries ago by Signora Pinetti and her husband Cavaliere Pinetti, who called himself a professor of natural magic. The royalty of several countries watched in amazement as the blindfolded *signora* named card after card drawn from a deck by her husband. She could identify the cards of the whole deck, because they were arranged in an order that she knew by heart.

A modern version of the trick is simpler. There is less memorizing; there is no confederate; and the performer's motions are easy and natural, leading audiences to think they may actually be witnessing a demonstration of telepathy.

The modern performer takes a deck of cards and spreads them out in a fan, face down. A spectator selects a card, looks at it, lays it face down on the table, then goes off to a corner to draw a picture of the card. Meanwhile the mind reader, in another corner, tries to pick up the spectator's thought waves and draw a picture from them. When the two pictures are compared, they show the same card.

Could this be television without a TV set? The real secret is that the cards have been arranged in a recognizable order. After the spectator has picked a card, the performer takes up the cards that had been lying above it and puts them under the rest of the deck. Now the bottom card is the one that had been just above the selected card. Stealing a glance at it, and remembering the order of the deck, the performer easily identifies the selected card.

31

The order of cards goes as follows, with a nonsense jingle for remembering it:

Eight kings threatened to save

8   K   3   10   2   7

ninety-five ladies for one sick knave.

9   5   Q   4   1   6   J

(Knave is an old word for the jack.)

In arranging the suits, the performer uses the word CHASED—C for clubs, H for hearts, S for spades, and D for diamonds. With this system, the deck begins: 8 of clubs, king of hearts, 3 of spades, 10 of diamonds, 2 of clubs, and so on.

In stacking the deck, the cards are laid down in the above order, face up; then, when turned over, they are in proper sequence for the trick.

When the performer peeks at the card that was above the selected card, the word CHASED is his key to the suit of the selected card, and the jingle is his key to the particular card of that suit. For example, if the 7 of spades is the card he glances at, he knows that the selected card is the 9 of diamonds.

This trick is stunningly effective. End your act with it. By now you have convinced people that you are a master mind reader—or that you can put on a good show.

3. PREDICTING THE UNPREDICTABLE

If you like a good, hammy role, be a prophet. Not a serious, straight-faced one, but a prophet with a light touch. Comedy won't hurt the tricks at all. In fact, a funny introduction helps. It throws people off guard; then they are all the more surprised when a prediction comes true.

As a funny phony seer, give yourself an appropriate name. Be Yogi Yogurt or Lotta Baloney. If you like, wear a costume. Spring an occasional gag, pun, catch, or corny joke. You learned a lot from Sir So-and-so. In England they said his magic was smashing. He turned his car into a lamppost. That was easy. But do you know the hardest thing he ever had to deal with? An old deck of cards.

Prediction tricks with comedy are great for parties. Fun starts right away, and keeps up as you do one trick after another without letting the audience in on how they work. Or if you decide to have audience participation, present the tricks as puzzlers. All of them are explained in the text or in Aftermath. So you can act very superior as your friends try to figure out why the predictions come true. Announce that the person who is the best problem solver will receive the magician's special prize, and at the end of the act award the winner a two-hundred-piece breakfast set: a box of cornflakes.

Prophet Without Honor

To set the mood for the first trick, which is an outrageous hoax, you might spring this old catch: Take two packs of cards (or two boxes of paper clips or toothpicks). Give one to your victim and keep the other. Turning your back, say, "Hold as many as you wish in one hand. No matter how many you take, I predict that I'll have more in my hand than you will." And of course you do, for your friend has none in *your* hand.

35

Answer the groans by saying, "A prophet is without honor in his own country. So you don't think I am a prophet. Well, I'll show you." Then announce you will predict the total of ten numbers, unknown to you, which the audience will choose. Make a big show of writing down your prediction, but keep it secret. Then call for numbers—two-digit numbers, for simplicity. Write each on a separate slip of paper, fold it and toss it into a hat. When you have ten numbers, pick two volunteers to be tellers. Each takes half the slips from the hat and adds the numbers—on a calculator if one is handy. Then the tellers add their two sums for the grand total.

One teller announces the total; the other reads your prediction. The two numbers are the same. Take a bow, prophet.

The trick is simple. When the first number is called—23, let's say—you put it down. But instead of writing the second number called, you write 77, so you have a pair adding up to 100. By doing this with four pairs of numbers, you reach a total of 400. Then comes the ninth number, which you record. But in place of the tenth, you write the number that will give the predicted total, which is 400 plus the last two numbers.

You needn't fear that the hoax will be exposed. The audience will trust the tellers. By the time the slips are taken from the hat, the tellers, like everybody else, will not remember all the numbers called out. Something is fishy, but since the numbers are all jumbled together, no one will be able to tell how you put over the trick.

A Total Mystery

Dice are used in this trick, giving you an opening for a gag. "Have you ever heard of number cubes?" you ask. "They are soap cubes marked with dots, like dice. Well, I was so good at dice, some people thought I cheated. So they had me use number cubes. They thought the soap would clean up the game."

To show your skill with dice and numbers, you propose to get the total of five numbers that turn up, without seeing all the numbers. Then this is what you do.

Hand three dice to a volunteer, Joan, and turn your back. Following the instructions you give her, Joan rolls the dice and records the three numbers on top in a column. Let's say they are 6, 5, 4.

For the fourth number, Joan picks up one of the dice—say it shows 6—looks at the bottom, and records the number there: 1.

Then she rolls that same die again and records the number on top: 2. This completes her column.

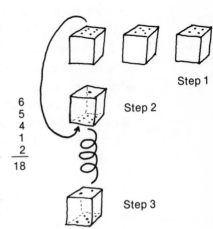

Step 1

6
5
4
1
2
—
18

Step 2

Step 3

When you turn around, the numbers on top of the three dice are 2, 5, and 4. From them you know the total of Joan's five numbers and you announce it: eighteen.

How did you get it? The two numbers you lacked were on the die Joan rolled twice. They were on opposite sides, so their total had to be seven, which is always the total of the numbers on the opposite sides of a die. Knowing this, you just add 7 to the three numbers you see: 2+5+4+7=18.

Calendar Caper

S	m	T	W	Th	F	SAT
	1	2	3	4	5	6
7	8	9	10	11	12	13
14	15	16	17	18	19	20
21	22	23	24	25	26	27
28	29	30	31			

"Your days are numbered," you remark, showing the audience a calendar. Invite someone to pick a month and draw a square around sixteen dates. Then announce that if four numbers within the square are chosen by people in the group, you will predict their sum even before the numbers are selected. So saying, write your prediction on a card and set it aside.

The volunteers select their numbers in the following manner. Someone makes the first choice, circles his number, and strikes out the rest of the column in which it appears, and also the rest of the row. Someone else circles a number that has not been crossed out, and strikes out the rest of that column and row. A third volunteer does likewise with a third number. Let's say they circle 10, 16, and 25 and the square looks like this:

The only number that has not been circled or struck out is 1. A fourth volunteer takes this number, adds it and the three encircled numbers, and finds that the total is 52. Whereupon you show the card with your prediction. It is . . . 52.

How do you do it? You just take the smallest number in the square, multiply it by 4, and add 48. In our example, where 1 is the smallest number, 4×1=4 and 4+48=52. This method never fails. Test it with various calendar squares and numbers and you will always get the correct total.

**FOR
PUZZLE
FANS**

Uncanny? Not if you use algebra to explain the trick. Let x equal the smallest number in the calendar square, and work out values for the other numbers. Now perhaps you can figure out why the trick works. For help, see Aftermath, page 119.

Reading with a Third Eye

This stunt gives you a chance to make a few cracks about math. It can be performed anywhere but is funniest in a math class, where everyone has the same textbook and can check on what you pretend to read from the closed book.

You have prepared a "third eye" in advance—an eye drawn on paper—which you now stick on your forehead.

"I can read hidden things with my third eye," you explain. "Some of the prophets of ancient Egypt had a third eye, and that's why they could see into the future. Anyway, that's what my mummy told me."

Holding up the math book, you ask the audience to think of the pages they want you to read from. A volunteer, Lou, goes around the room collecting page numbers from various people. He takes down one number at a time on a slip of paper, folds it, and tosses it into a hat. After ten or more numbers have been collected, you draw a slip from the hat. Holding it, still folded, close to your third eye, you announce the page number. Sure enough, your eye reads it correctly.

As the audience turns to that page, you hold the closed book up to your eye and give some of the text with a zany comment. A few more times, you draw slips and "read" from the closed book; then you can say your eye is getting tired.

How do you do this miraculous "reading"? Well, Lou is a confederate. You and he decide in advance on just four page numbers to be used. He writes only those numbers on the slips, disregarding the actual requests from the audience. The four numbers are repeated as often as necessary. For each of the four, the confederate folds the slip in a particular way. One is folded once, another twice, and so on. Just by noting the way a slip is folded, you know the number on it.

The remarks for each page are also prepared in advance.

For a page dealing with fractions, you mention one of the problems there, then you might add: "That's the sort of problem Liz So-and-so has trouble with, because she thinks four half shoes equal one pair."

For a page on the metric system, your crack might be: "Too bad for Dan So-and-so. He doesn't know anything about liters except that if you drink one half liter of milk a day for over fifty years, you'll live to be more than fifty years old."

For a problem on measuring an area: "Who asked for this page! I know Jack So-and-so didn't. He doesn't need any help with that kind of problem. He gets it wrong all by himself."

And for a page on equations or the commutative law: "Our class president knows $2000 \times 1 = 1 \times 2000$ but can't figure out why a politician kissing 2000 girls in 1 hour doesn't equal a politician kissing 1 girl for 2000 hours."

At the end, when you take off your third eye, remark that it is very nearsighted. It has to go to the eye doctor. You can add, flipping the pages of your math book, "Poor old book, it has problems too."

The Seer's Card Appears

As a warm-up for this trick, you hand a deck of cards to a volunteer—Tom, this time—and say, "Pick a card, remember it, and put it back. Now let me have the deck and I'll give you your card." Whereupon, you hand him the whole deck.

Ignore the groans and start the trick. "Willy-nilly," you say, "Tom will turn up a card that I predict." Have him shuffle the deck. You cut it and, as you do, you peek at the bottom card. Suppose it's the 3 of clubs; you write that down as your prediction. Next have Tom deal out twelve cards, face down. Then he is to turn up any four of them and put the remaining eight at the bottom of the deck. Say he turns up:

Tom now counts out cards, face down. For each face-up card, he deals the number needed to bring its value up to ten. He deals seven for the 3; one for the 9; nine for the ace; none for the jack, since a face card counts as ten.

Point out that the total value of the four cards is 23. Have Tom count off 23 cards from those remaining and show the 23rd to the audience. It is the 3 of clubs. Then your prediction is read—"3 of clubs"—to the wonderment of all.

FOR PUZZLE FANS

Can you figure out why the procedure in the trick leads to the seer's card.

For the solution, see Aftermath, page 122.

41

Tapping the Hours

To start this trick, hold up a stick and tell your audience that it is a divining rod for numbers.

"The stick is named Nimble,
Because it's so quick.
Think of a number, and
It finds the one you pick."

As you talk, draw a large clock face on a blackboard. Ask a volunteer—John, this time—to choose a number on the clock, write it down, and show the number to the audience but not to you. Explain that you will go around the clock, tapping on various numbers until the rod finds the one John has chosen.

While the tapping goes on, John's back is turned. He just listens counting the taps this way: To the first tap, he gives the value of his chosen number plus 1; then he adds 1 for each tap that follows until he reaches the count of 20. John's number, let us say, is 9. He counts the first tap as 10, the second 11, and so on. When his count gets to 20, he calls, "Stop." Turning around, he finds that Nimble is on his chosen number, 9.

How do you manage to have the stick there when John's count reaches 20? Or, putting it the other way around, how does it happen that John's count ends when the stick reaches the right number?

Well, you do some counting too. For the first seven taps, you hit numbers at random, but when you come to the eighth tap, you hit 12 on the clock face and count that tap as 12. From there on, you move the rod counterclockwise, counting backward with each tap—11, 10, 9—and then you hear John call, "Stop."

The drawing shows how the counting goes. John's count is circled. Yours is in the angles. For convenience, the first seven taps are shown as made from 1 to 7 on the clock. Actually, they can be made anywhere. But the counting backward from 12 must go in order, counterclockwise. The result is unfailing. At the end of John's count, your stick is on his chosen number.

Why this surprising outcome? In an old handbook, *The Secrets of Ancient and Modern Magic, or the Art of Conjuring Unveiled,* the reader is told, "The secret is so well disguised that it is very rarely discovered." Perhaps the author himself did not discover it, for he ends by saying, "The arithmetical reason for this curious trick, though simple enough in itself, is somewhat difficult to explain on paper, and we shall therefore leave it as an example for the ingenuity of our readers."

FOR PUZZLE FANS

Well, why not test your ingenuity?

To begin with, notice that John's chosen number, 9, when subtracted from 20, gives 11—the number of taps required to reach 9 on the clock. What happens if some other number—say 8 or 7—is chosen? You will find that no matter what number it is, subtracting it from 20 always gives the number of taps required.

Why? If you give up, see Aftermath, page 121.

Domino Divination

Nothing can be hidden from you, the seer. Let a domino be selected behind your back; you will tell which one it is. Not by sneaking a look in a mirror, nor by getting signals from anybody. You will do it with mathematics.

Who will pick the domino? Claire volunteers, and you tell her to choose a domino with dots on both halves. Say it is the 3/2 domino. Then, following your instructions, she does these calculations:

First she multiplies one of the numbers on the domino by 5.	3
	$\times$ 5
	15
Next she adds 7 to the product.	$+$ 7
	22
Then she doubles the sum.	$\times$ 2
	44
Finally, she adds the other number on the domino.	$+$ 2
	46

When you ask Claire for her result, she says, "Forty-six."

"I am seeing spots," you say. "They are the dots on a domino, and that domino is the 3/2."

How do you get it? You take Claire's result and subtract 14.

$$\begin{array}{r} 46 \\ -14 \\ \hline 32 \end{array}$$

The two digits in 32 cue you as to the numbers of dots on the chosen domino.

Try it with any domino with dots on both halves, and you find that the trick always works.

FOR PUZZLE FANS   The trick hinges on two unknown numbers. Can you figure out the mathematics involved in solving this type of problem? In other words, why does the trick work?

For an explanation, see Aftermath, page 122.

Egg Eggstraordinary

In other tricks you got predicted numbers from dice, dominoes, cards, a calendar, a clock. In this one you get the number from—no kidding—a hard-boiled egg. At the proper moment, a volunteer shells the egg and finds, plainly marked on it, the predicted number.

To prepare the egg, dissolve a teaspoonful of alum in one third of a cup of vinegar. With a small brush, which you dip in this solution, paint the number on the eggshell. When it has dried, boil the egg for fifteen minutes. Then keep it refrigerated.

This remarkable egg will need an introduction. Where did you get it? From an uncle of yours, an old magician. It was laid by his hen. The hen wanted to be pulled out of a hat, like a rabbit. The magician wouldn't do it, so the hen got mad and laid a hard-boiled egg. "Okay," said the magician, putting the egg aside, "if that's how you feel, lay a dozen. Do you hear me —the number I want is 12." But the hen misunderstood, it seems. She laid just one egg. The magician picked it up, saying, "Look, I want 12." He shelled the egg anyway and discovered, plainly written on it, a big, clear 12.

The magician was overjoyed. "Hen," he said, "if you can lay more eggs like this, we'll get rich and famous." The hen laid more eggs, and the magician eggsperimented with them. Finally they got it worked out so that each time the magician held an egg and called a number, that number would appear inside the egg.

Ending your story, you can say, "This egg is one that my uncle gave me. If someone will volunteer for the demonstration, he can hold the egg and see if it gives a number that he wants."

45

Ted volunteers and takes the egg. You tell him to pick any number between 20 and 100.

"Well, Ted, have you picked a number? All right, do this. Add the two digits. Subtract the sum from the number. The result has two digits. Add them. Don't tell me their sum—whisper it to the egg. Now shell the egg."

Ted shells the egg and finds, plainly inscribed on it, his final number: a big 9.

Suppose the number Ted started with was 71. Then the math would go like this:

Adding the digits $7+1=8$

Subtracting their sum
from the chosen number $71-8=63$

Adding the digits in
the result $6+3=9$

Try it with other numbers between 20 and 100, and you will always end with 9. Eggsactly.

FOR PUZZLE FANS

It's true that a hard-boiled egg is hard to beat. But why is the final number in the calculation always 9?

Remember that, in writing numbers, each digit has place value. And if that isn't enough of a hint, see Aftermath, page 125.

4. TEN WAYS TO MAKE PEOPLE THINK YOU ARE A GENIUS

Multiply in your head 5,645,418,496 by 1,338,978,361. Quick!

Is this asking the impossible? Well, William Klein multiplied the two numbers and got the right answer in just sixty-four seconds. At the European Nuclear Research Center, where he worked, staff members said he often solved problems faster than their giant computer.

As a youth, Klein put his talent to use in a traveling show. Billed as "The $50,000 Brain," he amazed audiences with his feats of lightning calculation. As far as is known, he is the only math wizard of this century who has used his talents for public entertainment. In the nineteenth century, however, a number of people who were lightning calculators gave exhibitions and went on tour. In Europe and also in the United States, people eagerly paid to see them perform.

Most sensational of the lightning calculators was Inaudi of Italy. He would subtract one 21-digit number from another, add five numbers that were each six digits long, multiply one 4-digit number by another, extract the cube root of a 9-digit number, find the fifth root of a 12-digit number, tell the number of seconds in a given period of time, and wind up by figuring out the day of the week of some historic date—all in twelve minutes!

Performances like that gave magicians the idea of imitating lightning calculation. Before long, they were beating the real math wizards at their own game. Or so it seemed, because their tricks were clever and because, as actors, the magicians put on a good show.

For dramatic effect a performer sometimes used a human skull, saying that it once held the brain of a great mathematician. When a problem was to be solved, the magician called upon the spirit of the dead genius for help. In response, the jaws of the skull (controlled by invisible threads) would move, and the magician pretended to hear the answer.

Other magicians worked without props. Claiming to be math wizards, they added, subtracted, multiplied, and divided at record speed. Audiences had no way of knowing that the problems were rigged. Even college audiences were fooled.

Nowadays, thanks to the pocket calculator, anybody can do rapid calculation. Push a few buttons and, presto! you have the answer to a problem that might take a quarter of an hour to solve with pencil and paper. But, fast as it is, the electronic calculator cannot beat a performer doing a rigged problem.

This makes the old tricks more surprising than ever. Several are described here, along with new twists and patter. When you perform, someone in the audience can use a calculator—if the numbers in the problem are not too large for it—and you will beat the calculator every time. Besides, you can handle very large numbers. Nine digits, eighteen digits, it doesn't matter. You solve all problems at lightning speed.

So, now to be a genius—the easy way.

Beat the Calculator

In this contest between you and a calculator, Sally offers to work the calculator. Explain that a column of ten numbers is to be added. A volunteer goes up front to write down the numbers on a blackboard, so the audience can add and check them too.

"Use any number to start with," you say.

The volunteer decides on 3.

"Now put down any other number."

The volunteer puts down 2.

"For the third number, use the sum of the first two."

Down goes 5 on the blackboard. 3

"For the fourth number, add 5 to 2." 2

Down goes the sum. 5

"Continue by adding each new sum 7
to the preceding one." 12

The volunteer stops after getting a 19
column of ten numbers. 31

"Okay, Sally, add them." 50

Sally starts pushing buttons on the 81
calculator, but before she gets very 131
far, you call out the total: 341. ___

How do you beat the calculator? You just take the seventh number, 31, and multiply it by 11. This is easy to do if you first, multiply 31 by 10 and then add 31 to the product:

$$(31 \times 10) + 31 = 341$$

FOR PUZZLE FANS

(1)	x
(2)	y
(3)	$x + y$
(4)	$x + 2y$
(5)	$2x + 3y$
(6)	$3x + 5y$
(7)	$5x + 8y$
(8)	$8x + 13y$
(9)	$13x + 21y$
(10)	$21x + 34y$
	$55x + 88y$

The trick always works. To prove it, let x equal the first number chosen, and y the second, and write the whole series algebraically. Note that the seventh number is $5x+8y$. Multiply it by 11, which gives $55x+88y$ — the right total.

It's also possible to get the right total as soon as you know the first two numbers. Can you figure out how?

For help, see Aftermath, page 123.

Backward Arithmetic

It is one thing, you tell your audience, to do a series of operations in your head and get the result. It is quite another to be given only the result of someone else's operations and work backward to the beginning. You can do this, too.

When you call for a volunteer, Carlos responds.

"Think of a number, Carlos, but don't let me know what it is. Take a nice, big one, because you will be using the calculator."

Carlos says he has decided on a number. At your suggestion, he writes it down and shows it to the audience so they can be in on the calculating.

"Ready, Carlos? Subtract 1 from your number; double the remainder; take away 1; and finally, add the number you started with. What is your result?"

Carlos says, 19368.

"Then," you tell him, "you must have started with 6457."

Yes, the wondering Carlos admits, that was his number.

These were his figures:

$$
\begin{array}{r}
6{,}457 \\
-1 \\
\hline
6{,}456 \\
\times 2 \\
\hline
12{,}912 \\
-1 \\
\hline
12{,}911 \\
+6{,}457 \\
\hline
19{,}368
\end{array}
$$

How do you "work backward" to the original number? This way: add 3 to the final result, then divide by 3.

$$19{,}368+3=19{,}371$$
$$19{,}371 \div 3 = 6457$$

Your Marvelous Memory for Numbers

To perform your mathematical feats, you need a prodigious memory for numbers. At least, that is what you tell your admiring victims. And then you give them a demonstration.

Show a list of five numbers, each of which is twenty digits long. Let somebody ask for any number on the list, and you will scribble down that number exactly, with every digit correct.

Here are some sample numbers:

(1)   91011235831459437077

(2)   02246066280886404482

(3)   12358314594370774156

(4)   22460662808864044820

(5)   32572910112358314594

Let's say you are asked for number 5 on the list. Without hesitation, you write it down, digit for digit, from beginning to end.

What is the secret of your marvelous memory?

Since you were asked for number 5, you add 18 to 5, which gives you 23. Turn it around, and you have the first two digits, 3 and 2. Add them to get the third. Add the second and third to get the fourth, the third and fourth to get the fifth, and so on. When you get a two-digit sum, just use the second digit.

The pattern is the same for each number on the list. For number 1, 18+1=19; and 19 reversed gives 91, and so on.

When you do the trick, don't go on adding digits past the twentieth. If you do, you'll give away the secret.

Fifty-two at a Glance

For you, remembering a sequence of cards is no more difficult than remembering a string of numbers. In fact, you can remember the order of the whole deck after a quick look through it.

To demonstrate, have a volunteer, Jack, shuffle the deck and spread out the cards, face up. After you glance at them, Jack brings the cards together without disturbing their order. Then he turns the deck over.

"Let's start with half the deck," you say. "Jack, count off any number of cards under 26. Count out loud, please."

Suppose Jack counts off 10 cards.

"Now look at the next card. Is it the queen of hearts?"

Jack turns up the card; it is not the queen of hearts.

"Put it back on the deck, Jack. And put back the 10 cards you counted off. Let me try again. This time, pick a number between 26 and 52 and count them off."

Jack decides on 27 and counts off the cards.

"Is the next card the queen of hearts?"

No. Wrong again.

"Give me one more chance, Jack. Put the card back, and put back the ones you counted off. Now count off 17 cards, and do it carefully.

Jack counts them off.

"Now turn up the next card."

Jack turns it up; it is the queen of hearts.

In this case, the queen of hearts was the first card in the spread. When the cards are turned face down, it is on top of the deck. To see what happens to it, go through the steps of the trick in private with the queen of hearts turned face up.

After ten cards are counted off and put back on the deck, the queen is the tenth from the top. After 27 cards are counted off and returned to the deck, 17 cards are above it. Count off those 17 cards and there is the queen of hearts.

The math is simple. In doing the trick, you subtract the first number the volunteer counts off from the second number. The difference gives you the final count:

$$27-10=17$$

The Hundred-numbers Problem

Are you kidding? your audience wonders when you propose to add a hundred numbers instantly. Instantly? You have to show them.

Okay, what number will you start with? Somebody says 21. Then you propose to add, in your head, the hundred numbers starting with 21 and ending with 120.

After a second of trying to look like a genius deep in thought, you give your total: 7,050.

If the total is to be checked with a calculator, it will take quite a while. Even four calculators, adding twenty-five numbers each, will be much slower than you in getting the total.

How do you find the total so fast? By knowing this: the hundred numbers can be grouped in fifty pairs each of which has the same sum. In our example, the first pair is 21 and 120, and their total is 141. Other pairs, in order, are: 22 and 119, 23 and 118, and so on. Since there are 50 pairs, you just multiply 141 by 50.

Incidentally, the easy way to multiply a number by 50 in your head is to add two zeroes to it (which, in effect, is multiplying by 100) and then divide by 2.

FOR PUZZLE FANS

The trick is easy when you know how. But to work out the solution by oneself—that takes some real mathematical thinking. Nearly two hundred years ago, in a schoolroom in Germany, the teacher, wishing to keep the class busy, gave them the hundred-numbers problem. To her surprise, a six-year-old discovered the solution at once. He was Karl Friedrich Gauss, who was to become one of the great mathematicians of all time.

Well, maybe you really are a genius too. Can you figure out how to get the product of a hundred numbers in just one step?

For the solution, see Aftermath, page 112.

Getting Two Sums at Once

Adding a set of numbers in one's head is not too difficult, you remark, but you are going to handle two sets at once—and with some extra complications.

This is how the trick will go: Your back is turned to the blackboard as numbers are called out, and a volunteer writes them down in a column. To make things simpler for the volunteer and audience (and for you!), the column will be rather short—just ten numbers—and the first number will be less than ten. Each succeeding number will be larger than the one before it. The volunteer, when putting down each number, will find the difference between it and the preceding number and will put the difference down in a second column.

	First Column	Second Column
The audience, let us suppose, calls out the numbers given in the first column. The "differences" make up the second column.	5	
	8	3
	11	3
	19	8
	25	6
	31	6
	45	14
	65	20
	72	7
	81	9

As soon as the tenth number has been called out, you give the totals of both columns: 362 for the first and 76 for the second. Have a volunteer use a calculator and check the totals.

Getting the total of the first column is simple enough. As a number is called, the volunteer takes a little while finding the "difference" and recording it. This gives you time to add the number. You do the same with each succeeding number, and thus get the total of column one.

But what about your really surprising feat, getting the total of column two? The truth is, this is even simpler. You just subtract the first number in the first column from the last number in the same column (81—5=76).

A nice short cut, but why does it work? Well, play around with the numbers a little. Suppose you end column one with the fourth number, 19. In this case, subtracting the first number from the fourth gives 14 (19—5=14); and the total of the three "differences" is 14.

The differences add up, so that the difference between the first number and any later one must be the same as the sum of the differences between them.

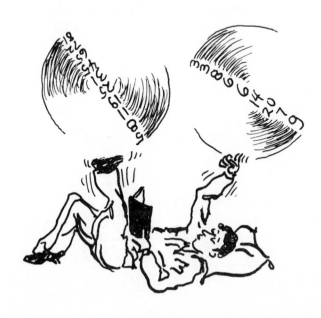

Day-of-the-week Reckoning

What day of the week was October 12, 1492, when Columbus landed in America? Imagine figuring that out in one's head in a few minutes! Yet many famous calculators could do it.

You, too, can solve a day-of-the-week problem.

Someone in the audience shows a large calendar and selects a month. This is done while your back is turned. You do not see the calendar, yet you will name the day on which the chosen month begins and the day on which it ends. All you need to know is the month chosen and the day of the eighteenth.

Suppose you are told the month is March and the eighteenth comes on Thursday. "Then," you say promptly, "the month begins on Monday and ends on Wednesday."

You get the answer by some backward and forward reckoning. Since the 15th of any month is the same day as the 1st, you reckon backward three days from Thursday the 18th. You find that the 15th is a Monday and the 1st is a Monday too. For the last day, you reckon forward. Since the 29th is always the same day as the 1st—Monday, in this case—you go forward two days from the 29th and find that the 31st is a Wednesday.

What else? You must know how many days are in each month. And watch out for February. If it is the chosen month, insist on knowing whether or not it is a February in a leap year.

March

SUN	MON	TU	WED	THR	FRI	SAT
	1	2	3	4	5	6
7	8	9	10	11	12	13
14	15	16	17	18	19	20
21	22	23	24	25	26	27
28	29	30	31			

Lightning Multiplication

Tell your audience you are tired of easy problems. Now you'll tackle a hard one: multiplication of two 9-digit numbers. The audience won't be able to use a pocket calculator this time; the numbers will be too large.

When you call for a nine-digit number, somebody proposes one—743,256,891, let's say—and you write it down on the blackboard. "Now for a multiplier. How about this?" you ask, casually writing 142,857,143 under the first number. You stand there for a moment, as if multiplying in your head. Then you put down the product, writing from left to right.

$$743,256,891$$
$$\times 142,857,143$$
$$\overline{106,179,555,963,322,413}$$

How do you find the answer? Not by multiplying, but by dividing. First, you imagine that the audience's number is repeated, digit by digit, to form an eighteen-digit number. Then you divide that number by 7. And that's it.

$$7/743,256,891,743,256,891$$
$$\overline{106,179,555,963,322,413}$$

Amazing, isn't it? But be prepared. If you are given a number that is divisible by 7, the product will be an eighteen digit number with the first nine digits repeated. "How extraordinary!" you say. "Strange things like that rarely happen."

FOR PUZZLE FANS

The trick works because the number you write down is a fraction of a certain 10-digit number. Can you figure out both the fraction and the whole number?

For the solution, see Aftermath, page 113.

Two Against One

In the next demonstration of your genius, you will multiply two pairs of four-digit numbers and add the products. All this in your head, of course.

Ask the audience for the first pair of numbers. Have one volunteer start multiplying them, then supply a pair of your own, and set another volunteer to work. Each can do the arithmetic any way he or she wishes—with pencil and paper, or on a blackboard, or with a calculator. Even if they both use calculators, you will beat them. Long before they have finished, you scribble down the answer.

How do you do it? The trick hinges on the numbers you supply. Your first number is made by subtracting the audience's first number from 10,000. For your second number, you use the audience's second number minus 1. Say these are the audience's numbers:

5329

7846

And this is the pair you supply:

4671

7845

After the multiplying and adding, this is the result:

78,455,329

How do you get it? By writing down the audience's second number minus 1, followed by their first number. And that's it!

Who says calculators work like magic? Magic is better—in this case.

FOR PUZZLE FANS

To understand the trick, go through the operations, using x for the audience's first number, y for the second, and xy for their product. Then your first number can be written 10,000—x; and your second number, y—1.

Multiplying your numbers:

$$
\begin{array}{r}
10{,}000-x \\
\times \quad\quad y-1 \\
\hline
-10{,}000+x \\
10{,}000y \quad\quad\quad\quad -xy \\
\hline
10{,}000y-10{,}000+x-xy
\end{array}
$$

Well, can you take it on from there? If you run into snags, turn to Aftermath, page 124.

Eighteen-digit Dazzler

In a final, splendid demonstration of your skill, you will take an eighteen-digit number and multiply it, in your head, by any number up to 18.

At your request, two persons from the audience volunteer to choose multipliers; they will also check your results. With pad and pencil, they prepare slips numbered from 2 to 18. The slips are mixed in a hat, then a volunteer picks one. Let's suppose it is 18.

What will you use as the eighteen-digit number? Going to the blackboard, you write, as if putting down digits at random:

$$526,315,789,473,684,210$$

"Multiplied by 18," you remark, and reel off the product, writing from left to right:
$$9,473,684,210,526,315,780$$

Your result is checked. Naturally, it is correct.

The procedure is repeated with a second multiplier, and again you quickly get the answer.

To succeed with the trick, you must be able to write out the eighteen-digit number. That's not hard. Memorize the beginning, 526,315. The next group, 789, is easy to remember. For the second half of the numbers, take the digits of the first half and subtract each in turn from 9.

How do you get your instant answer? First cut the long number into two parts, but watch where you cut. If the multiplier has only one digit, find the place in the long number where that digit is followed by a smaller one, and cut between the two. For example, with 7 as the multiplier, cut this way:

526,315,789,47/3,684,210

Next, transpose the two parts, placing the second part at the beginning and the first at the end. Then add a zero.

3,684,210,526,315,789,470

If the multiplier has two digits, consider only the second digit and find the place in the long number where that digit is followed by a larger one. With 18 as the multiplier, the cutting, transposing, and adding a zero gives:

526,315,78/9,473,684,210
9,473,684,210,526,315,780

And that's it!

After this trick, the climax of your brilliant performance, don't be surprised if your friends think you really are a genius.

FOR PUZZLE FANS

The key to the trick is an interesting fraction. When expressed as a decimal, the digits in it keep on repeating.

With this hint, can you figure out the fraction? If not, see Aftermath, page 114.

5. SPOOKY ARITHMETIC

Fakers known as mediums used to get rich by pretending to communicate with the dead. At the request of people who were mourning the loss of a relative or friend, a medium would prepare a séance. The affair took place in a darkened room, where the medium secretly produced strange sounds or lights to show that the spirit of the departed was present with a message for the living.

This practice began in New York State, over a century ago, when two sisters, Kate and Margaret Fox, became famous for their apparent ability to summon and talk with spirits. People who came to their demonstrations heard rapping sounds which did not seem to be made by any living person in the room. The rappings, the sisters claimed, were messages from spirits. Years later, they admitted having made the sounds by cracking the joints of their toes on the floor.

In spite of the confession of fraud by the Fox sisters, people continued to pay good money to attend séances. New techniques were developed to fool them. Mediums had messages appear on slates, or ventriloquized them, or produced them by so-called automatic writing. Each message seemed personal and genuine, for it included references to the customer's family history—information that the medium had picked up from old newspapers or tombstones.

At the end of World War I, mediums prospered by offering to communicate with the war dead. With séances becoming more and more popular, the magician Harry Houdini decided to investigate the business. He went in disguise to séances and became acquainted with the mediums' performances. Seeing a good way to get some publicity for himself, he offered a $10,000 reward to any medium who could produce an effect that he, Houdini, would not be able to duplicate. Then he put on a show of his own, contriving all the standard manifestations.

His exposés, Houdini thought, would convince everyone that mediums were frauds. He did persuade many of their followers, but not all. A few people were so impressed with Houdini's show that they decided that he himself was a medium. One man who believed this was Arthur Conan Doyle, author of the Sherlock Holmes mysteries. That's how good the tricks were!

Séance tricks are still good—but just for fun. Since many of them involve questions and answers, they can easily be combined with number problems. The magic that results, though funny, is just eerie enough to keep an audience on edge.

Try some of the samples of spookery that follow. Work them up one at a time and you will soon be ready to hold a math séance. For questions, you can use rigged problems, and for answers you can summon the ghost of a calculating genius, or the ghost of a magician. With such expert help, your answers will be correct—if you rehearse the tricks carefully.

Haunted Cards

QUESTION: What do you need when you go looking for ghosts?
ANSWER: You need a haunting license.

This old riddle makes a good opener for a program of Spooky Arithmetic. "Watch closely," you say, "and I'll show you the importance of a haunting license."

A helper is needed for your demonstration, and Josie volunteers. You hand her a deck of cards, then tell her what to do with them.

Following your directions step by step, Josie divides the deck more or less in half so there are two packets, each containing over 20 cards but not more than 29. She counts the cards in one packet. Let's suppose it contains 25 cards.

Josie announces the number and adds the two digits: $2+5=7$. At your request, she shows the seventh card from the bottom of the packet. It's the three of diamonds, let's say.

Josie puts the seven cards back on the bottom of the 25 *en* card packet and places this packet on top of the other one. Then she starts dealing off the top of the deck. Card by card, she spells out, "Y-o-u-r h-a-u-n-t-i-n-g l-i-c-e-n-s-e."

"Now," you say to Josie, "show us the last card you dealt."

Josie shows the card—it's the three of diamonds.

Very good! But what did the spelling of "Your haunting license" have to do with it?

These three words contain 19 letters. When Josie reaches the last letter—the 19th card—she has counted off 18 other cards. In the example given, she has reached the card that is 7th from the bottom of the 25-card packet. That's because $25-18=7$.

FOR PUZZLE FANS

Why does the trick work? Take any number in the twenties. Add its two digits and subtract the sum from the number you started with. The result, in every case, will be 18. Why 18?

Hint: the result is divisible by 9.

Give up? Then see Aftermath, page 125.

Houdini, Are You Here?

At Houdini's funeral, as friends of the great escape artist were carrying his casket, one whispered to another, "Suppose he isn't here."

After telling this story, announce that you are about to summon Houdini's ghost to assist with the next demonstration.

"Harry, Harry, Harry, are you here?"

A hollow, ghostly voice is heard (you ventriloquizing): "I am here."

You ask someone to take your deck of cards. Felicity volunteers. You tell her to pick any number up to twenty but keep the number secret from you. Then, as you direct her, she deals out three piles of cards. She deals the chosen number of cards on the first pile, the same number on the second, and eight cards on the third pile.

Following your instructions, Felicity gathers the three piles into one packet. She deals all the cards from the packet into two new piles: a card to the left, one to the right, and so on. Then Felicity picks up one of the two piles and deals off the unknown number she chose in the first place.

Now comes the question for the ghost.

"Harry, are you still with us?"

Ghostly voice: "I am here."

"Harry, how many cards remain in Felicity's hand?"

"Four."

Felicity counts out the cards: "One, two, three, four."

The trick is rigged so that the remainder is always half the number of cards in the third pile. The number does not have to be eight. Any number under twelve would do as well, provided that it be even. Try using an odd number and the trick will not work.

FOR PUZZLE FANS The trick is an old math problem in disguise. You can probably explain why it works. To check your solution, see Aftermath, page 122.

The Table Taps the Answer

The ghost who will assist with this trick can be a fictitious Greek mathematician, Calculobus. Introduce him as the genius who invented division—short, long, very short, and very long. In his lifetime he was a master of mental arithmetic, and he became still better at it after he died.

As the séance begins, you and three members of the audience sit around a card table. Everyone's fingertips are placed on the table. Lights are dimmed. This enables you to manipulate the table unobserved.

You: "I now summon the ghost of Calculobus. He will make his presence known by raising the table a little, then thumping it down on the floor. . . . Calculobus, give us a sign if you are here."

Up comes the table, then down it goes with a thump.

Calculobus is ready for the problem, which is: Can he tell at a glance if a number of several digits is divisible by 9? If it is, he will make the table thump three times for y - e - s. If it is not, he will thump twice for n - o.

Someone from the audience supplies a number—7453 for example—and almost immediately the table is felt to rise. Then come two thumps: n - o.

Someone else gives a number—8352, let's say—and the table promptly thumps y - e - s.

A quick check with a calculator shows the answers are correct.

In order to levitate the table, you need long sleeves. A ruler is strapped under each of your wrists. When placing your fingers on the table top, you slip the ends of the rulers under the table's edge. Then, by raising your hands a little, you can lift your side of the table off the floor. Lower your hands and the table goes down with a thump.

How do you quickly determine whether or not a number is divisible by 9? Just add the digits in the number, and if their sum is divisible by 9, so is the number. In the case of the number 8352:

$$8+3+5+2=18$$
$$18 \div 9 = 2$$
$$8352 \div 9 = 928$$

In the case of 7453:

$$7+4+5+3=19$$

$19 \div 9$ leaves a remainder

$7453 \div 9$ leaves a remainder

FOR PUZZLE FANS

Why does the rule for divisibility by 9 work? For the answer, see Aftermath, page 126.

Calling Calculobus

The lights are on as you say, "Now I shall call on the ghost of Calculobus to solve a different type of problem."

You take three dice and drop them into a glass jar. After shaking them up, you hand the jar to a spectator—to Josh. You tell Josh to look at the numbers on the bottoms of the dice.

"Don't let anyone else see the numbers," you say. "Just add them in your mind, and I'll ask Calculobus to tell us the total. Calculobus, are you here?"

A hoarse voice (your own) replies, "Here."

"Calculobus, what is the total of Josh's three numbers?"

A mumbling sound is the answer.

"Calculobus is speaking Greek," you explain. "He says the total is 9."

At your request, Josh lets people see the numbers on the bottoms of the dice. And indeed their sum is 9, for the numbers are: 5+3+1.

Wise, all-knowing Calculobus!

How do you get the total? Well, you know that the sum of the numbers on any two opposite sides of a die is 7. With three dice and three pairs of opposite sides to consider, the combined total is 21. Before handing the dice to Josh, you added the three numbers showing on top: 2+4+6=12. Then you subtracted: 21−12=9.

Spirit Writing

You: "Did you notice that Calculobus' voice was a little hoarse? It seems he has a cold, so let's not make him talk any more. Instead, I'll ask him to write the next answer."

You hold up a slate (or black cardboard) and a piece of chalk, saying, "That's for Calculobus. Now I just need a volunteer to give me a number—a number with three digits, all of them the same."

A volunteer supplies the number—555, let's suppose.

"I'll put it down," you say, "so Calculobus can see it. . . . Calculobus, please add the three digits, and divide the original number by their sum. Meanwhile, I'll wipe the slate clean so you can write the answer."

You pretend to wipe the slate clean with a handkerchief. Then you put down the slate and chalk and cover them with the handkerchief.

"Calculobus, Calculobus, have you written the answer?"

When you uncover the slate and hold it up, there, large and clear, is the number 37.

The volunteer checks with a calculator and finds that 37 is correct.

Of course, you never did write down the three-digit number. Instead, you wrote the answer, 37.

Will the result be the same with any three-digit number having identical digits? Try a few other numbers (in private) and you will find that the result is always 37.

FOR　　　Can you figure out how the trick works?
PUZZLE　　　Hint: It is a place-value trick.
FANS　　　If you give up, see Aftermath, page 126.

The Ghost Knows

You (sitting beside a covered table): "When Calculobus was living, no one spoke of ESP, but he probably had the gift. Shall we test him?"

For the test, you have prepared a set of twenty-one filing cards. These, you explain, are homemade ESP cards. Each is marked with a symbol, either 0 or 1 or 7, and each symbol appears on seven cards.

You fan out the cards, face down. A volunteer picks up three cards lying next to one another. What symbols are on the three cards? Ten different combinations are possible. So, naming the symbols on three cards takes a lot of luck—or a lot of ESP.

"Can Calculobus name the combination correctly?" you ask. "Can he write down the symbols that are on the three cards? . . . Calculobus, are you ready?"

With this, you show the slate, which is blank on both sides, and lay it on the floor under the table.

"Oh, yes, the chalk," you remark, and put that down too.

At your request, the volunteer shows the three cards with their symbols. There is one of each kind: 0, 1, and 7.

Now, what has Calculobus written?

You pick up the slate. And there, chalked upon it, are the three symbols: 0, 1, and 7.

The test is rigged, of course. The cards are arranged so that the three symbols come in a certain sequence, which is repeated over and over. As a result, any three neighboring cards have the three different symbols.

How did you write the combination on the slate? With your foot. You slipped your shoe off under the table. When pretending to lay down the chalk, you really stuck it between your toes.

Before the show, you had practiced writing with your foot until you were rather good at it. Houdini, by the way, was a good foot-writer. So were many mediums.

The Spook Takes a Hand

You: "This time, I'm going to ask the ghost of Calculobus to take my hand and make it write the answer to a problem. . . . Calculobus, Calculobus, please help me."

At these words, your hand, which is holding a pencil, jerks this way and that as if you were a robot. This shows that something, or somebody, has taken control of your hand.

"Now, who will give Calculobus a two-digit number ending with 5?"

"Thirty-five," someone suggests.

"Calculobus, how much is 35 times 35? Quickly!"

Your hand jerks up, jerks down, and writes a number: 1225.

Somebody fingers his calculator. Correct!

How do you get the number so fast? You just multiply the first digit by the next higher number and put down the sum. In this case, $4 \times 3 = 12$. Then you put down 25. The system works with any two-digit number ending with five. Try a few numbers (by yourself) and see.

FOR
PUZZLE
FANS
This is a place-value trick that is quite hard to figure out, but try anyway.
It is explained in Aftermath, page 127.

Who Did It?

Now for a sensational ending to your séance. For this trick you need ten small filing cards, which you number from 1 to 10. In preparing them, you first take a card and punch four holes near the upper edge. (If you don't have a punch, the holes can be made with the point of a scissors.) Then, using this card as a pattern, you mark the others through the holes and punch every card the same way. Next you cut through the tops of the cards in certain places to make open slits of the holes. When you have finished, your cards look like those in the drawing. Only one thing is needed besides the cards: a wire paper clip, straightened out.

When beginning the demonstration, you show the cards in numerical order, then shuffle them thoroughly.

"Now," you say, "I want to get the cards back in order, but without rearranging them myself. Instead, I will call for help from any ghost who may be in this room."

Holding up the packet of cards with the numbered sides toward you, and pointing the wire at it, you remark that you feel an unseen presence guiding your hand. Slowly, you stick the wire through the holes (or slits) on the extreme right. When you jiggle the wire a little, some of the cards come loose. Holding them together, you slip the other cards off the wire and put these in front. You even up the packet and repeat the procedure, sticking the wire through each of the other holes (or slits), one after another, from right to left.

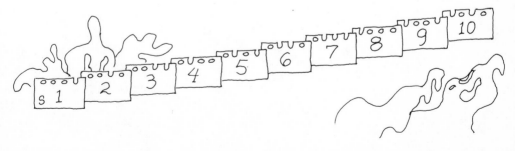

"The ghostly presence has let go of my hand," you say. "Now let's check the cards."

You fan out the cards, and there they are, in perfect order from 1 to 10.

Then you point out a letter appearing on the bottom of each card. Taken in order, the letters spell out: "SUPERGHOST."

"That's who arranged the cards!"

FOR
PUZZLE
FANS

Evidently, the holes and slits of the cards are some sort of code for the numbers 1 to 10. Can you decipher it?

If you need help, see Aftermath, page 116.

6. FORTUNETELLING WITH NUMBERS

Your friends are not superstitious, but just propose telling their fortunes and they are eager and ready. What does the future hold in store for them? This can be revealed, or so you claim, by time-honored methods involving the lore of numbers.

Long ago, only a few specialists could read and write and handle numbers. Not only were the specialists looked upon with awe, but the numbers themselves were revered too. The idea arose that numbers were magical—that they were endowed with powers affecting human lives. And this led to the belief that numbers could be interpreted as keys to the future.

Each of the digits from one to nine was supposed to possess its own special attributes. Borrowing from this tradition, you can make up your own code of number attributes.

1 – the source of all numbers, stands for reason.

2 – associated with the earth, earthiness, and female traits.

3 – an odd number, may denote the oddball, the original.

4 – stands for the square, symbol of justice and balance.

5 – stands for marriage, since it is the sum of 2, the first even or female number, and three, the first odd or male number after 1.

6 – the perfect number, symbol of perfection, since it is the sum of its three divisors $(1+2+3=6)$.

7 – the luckiest number.

8 – embodies the secret of love and friendship.

9 – promises wealth and plenty, since it is the largest of the digits.

This code can be helpful in several methods of fortune-telling. It can be used in evaluating the numbers on cards and coins and the numbers that are hidden in people's names. It may give you ideas for various plausible predictions.

What if you blunder with some incredible forecast? "No method is perfect," you calmly remark. You need not panic, as did the fortuneteller who told a woman she would lose her husband. When the woman said her husband had been dead for years, the fortuneteller blurted out, "Well, you're going to lose something—maybe an umbrella."

Of course, you will avoid remarks that might hurt someone's feelings. By keeping your patter light and breezy, you will be a great success as a fortuneteller. And that's one prediction you can count on.

What's in a Name?

The secret of one's future is hidden in one's name. Or so people thought long ago. The ancient Greeks and Hebrews used letters of the alphabet as numerals. Since A stood for 1, B for 2, and so on, writing a person's name was like writing a series of numbers. The name embodied a hidden key number, which was found by adding up the values of the letters. The bigger the total the more important the person would be. The Greek warrior Achilles was fortunate to have a name containing a higher total than the name of the Trojan Hector. This destined Achilles to be the greater hero, and so it turned out, for according to legend he won his fight with Hector.

Fortunetelling with numbers became known as numerology. Although few people believe in it any more, your audience will probably find it amusing to figure out the totals of their names and compare them. For their convenience, prepare a chart showing the values of all the letters from A to Z. Then let your friends go to work with pencil and paper and calculators.

Tradition dictates that persons with high key numbers are destined to be successful, but they can sometimes be tricked out of their good fortune. A name can be abbreviated or misspelled—a form of curse—to lower its value. This may even be tried by sneaky individuals in your audience. Others may seek to boost the value of their own names by adopting fancy spellings—for instance, Alyce instead of Alice.

The numerologists had another trick that seemed impressive in their day. If the total for a name turned out to have two or more digits, they added the digits to get a smaller number and, if necessary, added digits in the new total until they finally obtained a one-digit number. Doubly hidden, this was the secret, all-powerful key number in the name.

Consider how this procedure might work out for two members of your audience, named Ada Beam and Solomon Levy. Adding the values of their names, this is what you get:

A	1		S	19
d	4		o	15
a	1		l	12
B	2		o	15
e	5		m	13
a	1		o	15
m	13		n	14
	27		L	12
			e	5
			v	22
			y	25
				167

If 27 and 167 were the effective key numbers in their names, Solomon would seem to have a much more promising future than Ada. But see what happens when the totals are reduced to single digits. Ada's is reduced: 2+7=9. Solomon's is reduced: 1+6+7=14; and 1+4=5. Ada's 9, according to the number code you are using, portends wealth and plenty. Solomon's 5 portends marriage—a happy and enduring one, no doubt. So, as it turns out, Ada's and Solomon's futures are equally promising.

The Cards Will Tell

Cards were probably used for divination and fortunetelling before they were used for games. This seems likely when you consider how the card deck coincides with the calendar. There are fifty-two cards in the deck and fifty-two weeks in the year. There are four suits and four seasons. Putting the customary values on the face cards—king 13, queen 12, and jack 11—brings the total for the deck to 364, and a joker makes it 365, matching the 365 days in the year.

"Because the cards match the calendar," you tell your audience, "they can be used to predict when events will occur. My first demonstration will illustrate this. Who wants his fortune told?"

Joe does, so you hand him the deck and tell him what to do. Carrying out your instructions, Joe deals twelve cards, face down, in four rows. Then, while making a wish, he pulls a card from the deck, turns it face up, and places it on any card of the twelve. He repeats this with a second card from the deck.

"Well, Joe, what is your wish?"

"I'd like to make a lot of money," he says.

"Okay, let's see what the cards promise."

The first card pulled from the deck, the 2 of hearts, was placed by Joe on card number 1 of the twelve. His second choice, the queen of spades, was placed on card 3.

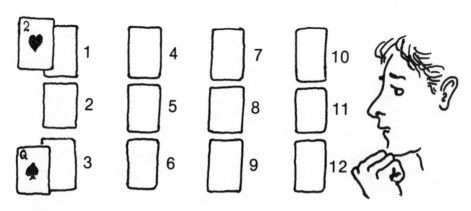

"The twelve cards stand for the months," you explain. "The first is January, so an important event in your life will happen in January. I can't be sure of the year, but I see the day. It is clear from your second chosen card. This card, the queen of spades, lies on position 3. I double 3 to 6, and add 6 to the value of the queen, which is 12. This gives 18, which means that the 18th of January is the date when the big event will take place.

"The queen of spades is a dark lady, whom you will meet on a January 18th. Will you marry her? You probably will, and you should, for spades means she is a hard worker.

"What will you both work at? Going back to your 2 of hearts, 2 refers to the earth, and hearts to certain riches of the earth colored red. Copper? Tomatoes? You will get rich either at mining or farming, or dealing in mineral or agricultural products. Congratulations!"

Joe is pleased, for the forecast jibes with his two hobbies: gardening and rock collecting.

Who is next? Giving the others their turns, you make the fortunetelling impressive by always following the same general procedure, based on the standard meanings of numbers, cards, and card positions. Here are some plausible meanings:

for the face cards
   ace - high achiever
  king - a man
queen - a woman
  jack - a young man

for suits
   clubs - forcefulness
  hearts - friendliness, love
  spades - industriousness
diamonds - ability to make money

Of course, you won't stick rigidly to the scheme. You will use your wits, as you did with Joe's forecast, and contrive something suitable for each person. That's the best kind of fortunetelling!

Fateful Choice

To inspire confidence, work a good card trick into the show. People will feel that if you can identify a card without seeing it, you certainly can be trusted to divine its meaning.

In this feat you exhibit both abilities. You name an unseen card and tell a fortune from it. Whose fortune? Juliana's.

Juliana is given a deck and told to fan out the cards, face down. Then she picks up one of them without letting you see it.

"Your choice will reveal your fate," you say. "I think I can name the card you have chosen, but I need a little help from you. Would you please

        (1) multiply the value of the card by 2
        (2) add 3 to the result
        (3) multiply the sum by 5.
        (4) If the card is a club, add 1
            If it is a heart, add 2.
            If it is a spade, add 3.
            If it is a diamond, add 4.

Now, Juliana, please give me your result."

"Fifty-six," she says.

Staring into space, you declare, "I see a color—black. It is clubs. And the number is 4. The fateful card you have chosen is the 4 of clubs."

Juliana shows her card—the 4 of clubs.

How could you identify it? Not by knowing Juliana's arithmetic, which goes like this:

(a) $4 \times 2 = 8$
(b) $8 + 3 = 11$
(c) $5 \times 11 = 55$
(d) $55 + 1 = 56$

All you have to go by is the final number, 56. You subtract 15 from it: $56 - 15 = 41$. In this result, the digit at the right, the 1, is the key to the suit, according to the code:

Clubs — 1
Hearts — 2
Spades — 3
Diamonds — 4

The other part of the 41, the 4, gives the number of the card.

What does the 4 of clubs portend for Juliana? According to your reading, a reputation for forcefulness (clubs) in upholding justice (4).

"This," you tell Juliana, "means that you are destined to become a lawyer for important causes."

Could anyone doubt the reliability of your forecast?

FOR PUZZLE FANS

Of course, you will wonder why the trick works. If you can't figure it out, see the explanation in Aftermath, page 123.

Four at a Time

So as not to leave anybody out of the fortunetelling, you can make forecasts for four persons at a time. Suppose you start with Mary, Suzie, Mark, and Lou. You arrange them in that order, clockwise, with Mary at your left. You are number 5. You deal the cards clockwise, face down, five to each person, including yourself. Each one looks at his or her hand, mentally selects a card, to be remembered as favorite, and puts the hand down.

You gather the five hands, still face down, and stack them in order, with Mary's cards on the bottom and yours on top. Then you deal the cards again, five to each person, clockwise, from Mary around to yourself. You ask for a hand of cards, receive one from somebody, turn it over, and fan out the cards. Suppose the hand is:

"Does anyone see their card among the five?" you ask.

Mark says his card is there.

"I feel something," you say. "There are vibrations coming from the jack of clubs."

"Right," Mark says, "that's my card."

"Its message is clear," you tell him. "You will be a strong athlete, which I read from clubs, and you will become one when you are still young, which is the meaning of the jack."

If no one else's card is in this hand, you collect the cards and deal them again. Sooner or later all the chosen cards come up. Unfailingly, whenever someone says their chosen card is in a fan, you promptly identify the card.

How do you always identify the right card? Notice that Mark's jack of clubs was the third card in the fan. You identified it from its position, which, you knew, had to be the same as Mark's position in the order of dealing. The whole procedure guarantees that each chosen card will occupy the same place in the fan that its owner occupies at the table.

As you go on telling fortunes wholesale, you make four people happy, managing to discern something good in the cards for all of them.

FOR PUZZLE FANS   The principle of this trick is very well hidden. Can you find it? If not, turn for an explanation to Aftermath, page 118.

Birthday Magic Square

Because numbers were thought to control the future, people used to wear good-luck charms with numbers on them. One such charm was the magic square.

Your next demonstration will be to construct a personal magic square for someone in the audience. It will be made up of the numbers in his or her birth date. To remind everybody what a magic square is, show them the simplest one:

4	9	2
3	5	7
8	1	6

Point out that the sum of the three numbers in each column, and in each row, and in each diagonal, is the same: 15.

"This remarkable arrangement," you tell your audience, "endows the magic square with mysterious powers."

The first person to ask for a personal magic square is Evvie. Her birth date, she says, is February 5, 1970.

Using a big card or blackboard, you draw a square partitioned into nine boxes. For your own guidance, you have drawn a smaller square on paper and identified the boxes with letters in this way:

This is how you proceed, using Evvie's birthdate, 2/5/70, and entering the appropriate numbers in the proper boxes of the square on the blackboard.

A. In box A you write the year (70).

B. You add the date to the year (5+70) and put the sum (75) in box B.

C. You add the date to that sum (5+75) and put the new sum (80) in box C.

D. You add the month to the year (2+70) and put the sum (72) in box D.

E. You add the month to that sum (2+72) and put the new sum (74) in box E.

F. You add the month to the number in box B (2+75) and place the sum (77) in box F.

G. You add the month to that sum (2+77) and place the new sum in box G.

H. You add the month to the number in box C (2+80) and put the sum (82) in box H.

I. You add the month to that sum (2+82) and put the new sum (84) in box I.

Now all the boxes have numbers, but do they make a magic square? A few minutes' work with a calculator proves that they do. When the columns, rows, and diagonals are added up, the sum in each case is 231. Reducing this number to a single digit (2+3+1=6) gives Evvie the perfect number, 6, which, according to ancient lore, means that her personality and prospects are . . . perfect!

Oriental Coin Toss

The method of prediction you will now demonstrate, you can tell your audience, is derived from the ancient Chinese system called I Ching. Remarkably, the 2000-year-old I Ching closely resembles the modern binary system used in computers. Two symbols are employed—not the 0 and 1 of the binary system, but a broken line and a whole line. These lines are arranged in 64 combinations, which correspond to the first 64 numbers of the binary system. (For a table of binary numbers, see Aftermath, page 115.)

Fortunetelling with the I Ching was a complicated procedure. A set of 50 sticks had to be divided and subdivided over and over in order to construct combinations of symbols. The ritual took a long time, and this cut down the number of fortunes that could be told in a day and the number of fees that could be earned.

How could fortunetelling be speeded up? Certain practitioners found a way. Giving up the wearisome ritual with the sticks, they substituted coin tossing. Then the finding of symbols was quickly determined, by the heads and tails that turned up.

Concluding this story of the Chinese fortunetellers, you come to the matter at hand. You yourself will tell someone's fortune with an oriental coin toss—your own quickie method of I Ching. But in your version, the symbols will be the 0 and 1 of the binary system.

Who wants his fortune told? Larry does.

You give Larry six coins. All he has to do is shake them and let them fall. Then you, with your eyes closed, arrange the coins in a row. They happen to line up in this order of heads and tails:

T H T H T T

You ponder the result for a moment and then announce, "Larry, you are fortunate indeed. The coins guarantee you the best possible future, for they give you the lucky number 7.

As you then explain, heads stands for 0 and tails for 1, so Larry's coin order translates into:

1 0 1 0 1 1

This binary number is the same as 43 in the ten-based system. And 4+3=7.

Lucky Larry!

The Futurescope

An amazing instrument, the futurescope, makes it possible to combine fortunetelling with mind reading. The scope detects questions and answers that people have about the future.

Make your own futurescope by copying these four circles. You will also need a list of fifteen numbered questions, written on a large card. You can make up your own questions or use those suggested on page 97. In any case, choose questions that lead to zany answers—the zanier the better.

Tell your audience that the futurescope is designed to handle the fifteen questions people most commonly ask. "Though it looks simple," you remark, "the scope works on a complicated principle. It picks up certain Q vibrations affecting a person's future, and I decode the vibrations."

Beginning your demonstration, you ask someone from the audience—Noah, let's say—to select a question from the list. He is not to let you know which one he chooses but is to touch all the circles that contain the number of his question.

Suppose Noah touches the first, second, and fourth circles (in order from left to right). You promptly say, "Your question is number 13 on the list: Will I make a lot of money? The answer is, yes, if you work at the mint."

After answering Noah's question, you can do the same for other persons in the audience. You read the question in each one's mind correctly, and give an enlightening answer.

Note: The answers are suggestions for you. Do not put answers on the list of questions to be used by the audience.

1. How can I get ahead?
   From a head-hunter.
2. How many children will I have?
   Any number from zero on up.
3. Whom will I go around with?
   Someone you will meet in a revolving door.
4. Will I get fired?
   Only if you're an elevator operator and can't remember the route.
5. How can I prove I'm right?
   Are you, if it's so hard to prove?
6. When will I get married?
   After the date is set.
7. How can I make my money go a long way?
   Send it abroad.
8. Should I bet on our school team?
   Only if the game is called off on account of rain.
9. Is there a sure way to make money on the state lottery?
   Yes. Sell tickets on commission.
10. When will I get a job?
    Right before your first pay check.
11. Will I be important and have a lot of people under me?
    Yes, if you work as watchman in a cemetery.
12. Should I sell my bike?
    No. Pay somebody to take it away.
13. Will I make a lot of money?
    Yes, if you work at the mint.
14. Should I offer sympathy to my friend?
    Why bother? Anyone can find it in the dictionary.
15. How can I make my girl friend (or boy friend) say, "Yes"?
    Ask your friend what y-e-s spells.

How do you always know what question has been picked? All you do is add up the numbers at the tops of the circles that are touched. Notice that these numbers are 8, 4, 2, and 1. They total 15, so if all the circles are touched, you know that the chosen question is number 15. In Noah's case, the top numbers were 8, 4, and 1, adding up to 13.

FOR PUZZLE FANS

Once again, the key to the trick is the binary system. With this hint, you can probably figure out why the trick works. To check your answer, see Aftermath, page 117.

7. CRAZY CALCULATING

A short, snappy comedy number adds sparkle to a magic show. It can serve as an ice-breaker, as a breather between acts, or as an encore. It can be worked into almost any type of program.

Certain classical tricks are easily turned into comedy—for example, sawing a lady in half, or baking a cake in a hat. And nothing makes better fun than mathematical nonsense. It can be strung together on a story line enlivened with gags and surprises.

The skits that follow will give you some ideas to develop in your own way. Several roles are suggested. You, the performer, become a stand-up comic, a ventriloquist, a cryptographer, a cook—whatever the material demands. But always you are a mathematician—of sorts.

Sawing a Lady in Half and Other Problems with Fractions

Holding a pointer, you the Professor stand before an easel with an art pad on it, ready to give a lecture on the arithmetic of sawing a lady in half. A drawing on the pad shows a long box with a girl's head sticking out from one end and her feet from the other.

Clearing your throat, you begin: "Sawing a lady in half is like other mathematical problems. Accuracy is required. If you make even a small mistake, the problem doesn't come out right, and neither does the lady."

Writing a big numeral 1 on the pad, you explain, "The lady, whom we call Unity, is expressed by the number 1. She is to be sawed, or fractured, into parts called fractions. Sawing her once yields two fractions, and the problem requires that they be equal—that is, halves. Each half is conventionally represented as . . ." and you write a "½" on the pad.

"Note this expression carefully," you go on, "for it describes what we do to Unity. The term above the line is the numerator. It tells how many parts of her are in the fraction. As you see, there is only one. The lower term, the denominator, tells how many equal parts Unity is fractured into. Two.

"If we follow these principles, the outcome of the operation is assured. Unity is sawed precisely in half.

"Her fractions, like the lady herself, are proper. By definition, a proper fraction is less than one. In former times, Unity's fractions would have been called vulgar. That simply meant they were written in the ordinary way—with a numerator and denominator separated by a line. Nowadays we say they are common fractions, which sounds better.

"The lady's fractions by themselves are not vulgar at all, though some of the remarks made about them by comedians are. For example, there is the gag that being sawed in half may cause a lady to speak broken English. Or cause her to have double vision. Then there is the joke about an unemployed magician who sawed a lady in half and couldn't make ends meet. But to return to our problem, you might ask why it is always a lady who is sawed in half. Why not a man? As a matter of fact, a man was used when the feat was first performed, in the 1920s. Ever since, however, magicians have picked women, or picked *on* women, because magicians have been men.

"What if we go back to using a man? A very interesting result is obtained if we saw a man in half as well as a lady. The man's fractions together equal 1, and the lady's also equal 1. Now, according to a well-known rule, if two quantities are equal to a third quantity, they are equal to each other. In the present case, the lady and the man both equal 1. Therefore, they are equal to each other. Consider the significance of this conclusion. It provides irrefutable mathematical proof that women are equal to men."

The Calculator as Lie Detector

"This wonderful instrument," you say, holding up a pocket calculator, "has capabilities that go beyond arithmetic. For example, it can be used as a lie detector."

By way of illustration, you tell the following story:

Barnabas Bell, the operator of a small circus, decided to make a week's stand in Hilltown, and saw the mayor about renting the fairground. After some bargaining, the two men agreed on a figure for the rental. It would be either $600 or 5% of the gate receipts, whichever amount was greater.

The circus played for a week in July to audiences from several counties. Then it moved, and everybody forgot about it. That is, everybody but Lem Nosey, publisher of the local paper. Suspecting some hanky-panky with money, he ran a story demanding an investigation of the deal between Barnabas Bell and the mayor.

An investigation was held. When the town records were examined, they showed that $600 had been received by the mayor as rent for the fairground.

Would the circus records confirm this?

Going on with the story, you use figures you have written down.

The circus records showed that gate receipts were $15,138, and 5% of that sum, $756.90, was paid as rent for the fairground. Total expenses:

Rent for fairground	$756.90
Advertising	2643.10
Operating expenses	4000.00
	7400.00

The town accountant checked the addition on his calculator, as you now do on yours. Then he subtracted the expenses from the total gate receipts:

Receipts $15,138
Expenses   −7400
            7738

Now, who, if anybody, was telling the truth about the rent paid?

With 7738 showing on your calculator, you turn it upside down and the audience reads the answer: BELL.

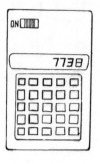

The mayor's bank account was examined next, and the figures went down on the accountant's calculator (as they now do on yours):

Balance as of July 1   73,500
Deposits in July   317
Balance as of July 31   73,817

Triumphantly, the mayor turned the accountant's calculator upside down (as you now do with yours) and exhibited the word: LIBEL.

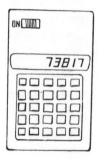

"That's what you are guilty of in slandering me," said the mayor. "It is libel."

But then the bank produced the mayor's deposit slips for July. There were two, and one of the deposits, curiously enough, was for $156.90—exactly the difference between what Barnabas Bell said he paid ($756.90) and what the mayor turned over to the town ($600). Summed up on the calculator, the two deposits came to:

156.90
160.10
317.

Was the mayor's statement about the rental a lie or the truth?

When the accountant turned his calculator upside down (which you now do), the mayor read the answer. Because of it, he decided to pay the town $156.90, resign from office, and retire to his farm.

The answer on the calculator was: LIE.

The Arithmetic Dummy

A skit about arithmetic can be presented in the form of a conversation between a ventriloquist and her dummy. If your dummy is homemade and his mouth doesn't move when he talks, but yours does, who cares? Just keep your lips slightly apart and try not to move them much.

The skit can go like this. Introducing the dummy, named Allie, you say, "This is Allie. He is in the class I teach, and he's pretty smart. Say hello to the people, Allie." Allie bows and says hello. Then comes this dialogue:

YOU: Tell the people something about yourself. Are you an only child?

ALLIE: Now I am. I used to be twins.

YOU: When were you twins?

ALLIE: When I was two.

YOU: You seem to like numbers. Can you count?

105

ALLIE: One, two, three, four, five, six, seven, eight, nine, ten, jack, queen, king.

YOU: Who taught you to count that way?

ALLIE: My father. He's a magician.

YOU: Can you count past ten?

ALLIE: With my shoes off.

YOU: With your shoes off?

ALLIE: Yes. Then I can count on my toes.

YOU: Good. Now let's see if you can solve a problem.

ALLIE: Okay.

YOU: If a man buys something for $12.25 and sells it for $9.75, does he gain or lose on the deal?

ALLIE: He gains on the cents but loses on the dollars.

YOU: Not bad. Now another problem. Jake and Charlie go to Georgia and buy a truckload of watermelons at a dollar each. Then they drive to New York and sell the watermelons for a dollar each. Jake counts the money. "We have $200," he says. "But we started with $200," Charlie says. "Something is wrong." Well, Allie, what's wrong?

ALLIE: They need a bigger truck.

YOU: Good boy! Next we'll do some division. I tear this paper in half, then tear the halves in two, and what do I get?

ALLIE: Fourths.

YOU: I tear the fourths in two and what do I have?

ALLIE: Eighths.

YOU: I tear the eighths in two and what do I have?

ALLIE: Sixteenths.

YOU: I tear the sixteenths in two and—

ALLIE: Thirty-seconds.

YOU: I tear the thirty-seconds in two and what do I have?

ALLIE: Confetti.

If people applaud, Allie bows; if they don't, he bows anyway.

Absent-minded Professor on the Telephone

The phone rings (a bicycle bell or doorbell). The Professor (you) comes in, wearing a bathrobe. He yawns and picks up the phone.

"Hello."

"Good morning," says a voice (you ventriloquizing). "Is this the bank?"

"No. You have the wrong number. This is Dr. Genius of the Math Department."

"Sorry."

"That's all right. The phone was ringing and I had to answer it anyway."

The Professor puts down the phone, then picks it up again. "That reminds me, I must call John. Now, what's his number? I should have it at hand. Hand, five fingers, five—that's the first digit. Five o'clock is when guests come. How many? Eight—the second digit. And what do they do? Eat. Eat, ate. Another eight. 588. Four more digits to go.

"How late do the guests stay? Until two-thirty. There are the next digits: two, three. John brings his wife, May. January, February, March, April, May—the fifth month. Five. May is funny, as funny as a three-ring circus. Three! Now I have it: two three five three."

Noticing his address book near the phone, the Professor picks it up, saying, "Oh, here's John's number, as plain as can be: 588-2353. Why, that's five million, eight hundred eighty-two thousand, three hundred fifty-three. How could I forget a number like that! It's one seventeenth of a hundred million and one!"

Then the Professor dials, muttering the number his way, "Five million, eight hundred eighty-two thousand, three hundred fifty-three."

A twangy voice comes over the line, "The number you are calling has been disconnected. This is a recording. The number you are calling . . ."

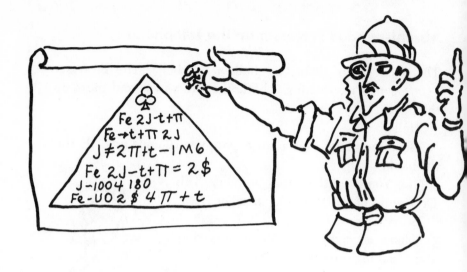

Mystery of the Pi Parchment

The renowned cryptographer Sir Jay Kidyou Knott (you) stands with pointer in hand before a large hanging scroll inscribed in the way pictured.

"This scroll," the cryptographer says, "is the mysterious Pi parchment, of Alexandria, Egypt. A collector found it in a shop there a few years ago. Classical scholars examined the parchment, argued and debated over it, and could agree only that it was a funerary text stolen from a tomb, possibly the tomb of a pharaoh. But the meaning of the text eluded them until I was called upon to unravel the mystery.

"The first thing that struck me about the scroll was the strange mixture of symbols. One is the Greek letter π, Pi, which is used as a mathematical expression. Some of the symbols are letters of the Roman alphabet. Others, I suspected, were numerals of unknown value.

"Searching for a key to the text, I asked myself, why were the lines contained in a triangle? And why was the first symbol a club? Suddenly, a possible explanation dawned on me. In Alexandria there was a restaurant called the Triangle Club, where I had eaten often. The text might be a record of some sort from the restaurant.

"Then it struck me there was something familiar about the style of the characters. I had seen this handwriting before, on checks written by my favorite waitress, Effie.

"Proceeding from this discovery, I was able to work through the whole document, line by line. With some embarrassment, I recognized that the text was a memorandum by Effie about an incident that had occurred between us. It can be transcribed as follows:

Line 1: Effie to Jay—'Tea and pie?'

Line 2: Effie brings tea and pie to Jay.

Line 3: Jay is not equal to tea and pie—'I'm sick.'

Line 4: Effie to Jay—'Tea and pie is two dollars.'

Line 5: Jay—'I owe nought for I ate nought.'

Line 6: Effie—'You owe two dollars for pie and tea.'

"And that," the cryptographer remarks in conclusion, "was the message of the scroll: I owed the Triangle Club two dollars. The next time I went there, I paid up and apologized to Effie."

You Bake a Cake in a Hat Using Metric Measurements

On the table before you are ingredients for baking, an electric hot plate, a wooden spoon, a hat, and a sifter. Nobody suspects that you have fixed aluminum foil under the sifter, so that ingredients put into it will not go through. Nor that the two eggs on the table are empty shells, which you have prepared by making holes in the ends and blowing out the contents. Nor that there is anything under the hat.

Standing with an open cookbook in hand, you mutter, "Hmm. This cookbook has metric measurements. Guess I can manage. Here's a recipe for a cake for eight, quick-mix method. But I need a pan 7×7 cm—seven by seven centimeters. I think that's the size of my hat. Okay, I'll use my hat."

You turn the hat up on the table and set the sifter in it. Then you go on reading from the recipe (your own, which you have taped into the book).

"Hmm. 250 ml—milliliters—of flour. That's a fourth of a liter. A liter is about a quart, and a fourth of a quart is a cup. Okay, one cup of flour."

You measure a cup of flour and pour it into the sifter.

"Now what? 200 ml sugar. That's not hard. If 250 ml is a cup —200 is four-fifths of a cup." Carefully, you measure the sugar and pour it into the sifter.

"Five ml baking powder. That's $5/250$, or $1/50$ of a cup—maybe a teaspoonful," and into the sifter goes the baking powder. "Now salt," you say, shaking some into the sifter.

Holding the sifter over the hat, you turn the handle around a few times, tap and shake the sifter a little as if to make sure it is empty, and set it aside.

"Oh, yes, the eggs," you remark, and break the prepared eggshells over the hat.

Stirring the ingredients that are supposedly in the hat, you take another look at the recipe. "Bake in a hot oven."

You set the hat on the hotplate, spend a little time cleaning up, then pause and sniff. "It smells finished already."

Gingerly lifting the hat as though it were a hot pan, you take it from the stove. Then you hold a plate over the hat and turn them over together.

When you remove the hat, there, on the plate, is a cupcake.

"What went wrong?" you exclaim. "Why is the cake so little? Oh, of course: centimeters are smaller than inches, and milliliters are smaller than cups!"

8. AFTERMATH

By now you have discovered that the tricks in this book contain more magic than math. What math there is rarely goes beyond elementary arithmetic—usually no farther than addition and subtraction. In some cases it doesn't even go that far; it is just a matter of counting, or remembering numbers, or picking up signals from a confederate. A few of the routines are simply hoaxes or strings of gags. At the other end of the scale of difficulty are tricks based on solving algebraic equations with two unknowns.

But difficult math is not needed to make a trick deceptive. After all, Dunninger's Brain Buster (page 21) is based on nothing more complicated than addition and subtraction.

Houdini once said, ". . . it is not the trick which impresses the audience, but the magician." And this is certainly true of number tricks. They seem quite varied because of the magic created by the performer's patter and misdirection. Yet many of them are fundamentally alike. Consider, for example, Telephoney (page 25), Egg Eggstraordinary (page 45), and Haunted Cards (page 70). One is mind reading, one is a prediction, and one is spookery, but the same math concept underlies all three tricks.

Strip away the magic from any real number trick and its true nature is revealed. At the heart of each one lies an arithmetic or algebra problem that is secretly solved by the performer. As you analyze the tricks in this book, you find a few types of problems appear again and again. In fact, only six types show up. They are based on:

1. Simple computation—addition, subtraction, multiplication, division
2. Repeating decimals
3. Binary numbers
4. Intersecting sets
5. Algebraic equations
6. Place-value concepts

In the following discussion, the tricks and puzzles dealing with similar problems are grouped together. The math involved in a type is explained first in general, then in particular as it applies to each trick and puzzle.

Even though the math in mathematical magic is fairly simple, you will find it is ingenious. In its own way, it is as fascinating as the magic.

Tricks and Puzzles Depending on Simple Computation

All the tricks in this category are explained in the directions for performing them. The only puzzle connected with this group (see page 57) asks how you can multiply a hundred numbers in one step. The answer: Make sure one of the numbers is zero.

Fractions and Repeating Decimals

A decimal is a fraction that is written with a decimal point followed by one or more digits. A repeating decimal is a special type in which a digit or a group of digits keeps on repeating. The best known example is .33333 . . . , which can also be written ⅓. The fraction ⅐ forms a decimal in which the digits 142857 repeat endlessly. Because of the repetition, this type of decimal is useful in certain number tricks.

LIGHTNING MULTIPLICATION (page 61) depends on the fact that the number you use as a multiplier—142,857,143—is one seventh of a billion and one. Now, when any nine-digit number is multiplied by a billion and one, the product is an eighteen-digit number whose first nine digits are the same as the second nine. Check this, using the number provided by the audience, and you get:

$$
\begin{array}{r}
743,256,891 \\
\times 1,000,000,001 \\
\hline
743256891 \\
000000000 \\
000000000 \\
000000000 \\
000000000 \\
000000000 \\
000000000 \\
000000000 \\
000000000 \\
743256891 \\
\hline
743256891743256891
\end{array}
$$

This is the secret of the trick. In effect, you multiply the audience's number by 1,000,000,001, then divide the product by 7. You would get the same answer if you actually multiplied by 142,857,143, since it is equal to ⅐×1,000,000,001.

By the way, notice the first six digits in the multiplier. All six keep on repeating when ⅐ is written as a decimal.

EIGHTEEN-DIGIT DAZZLER (page 64) In this feat of lightning calculation, you multiply any number from 2 to 18 by this number:

526,315,789,473,684,210

The key to the trick is the fraction $\frac{1}{19}$. When expressed as a decimal, it is made up of this group of 18 digits that keep on repeating:

.052631578947368421

Compare this decimal with your eighteen-digit number and you see they are related. In both numbers, the same digits occur in the same order, except for the zero. In the decimal, the zero is in the first place. Transpose it to the last place, remove the decimal point, and you have your eighteen-digit number. This number turns out to be equal to $\frac{10}{19}$ of one quintillion (1,000,000,000,000,000,000) minus one, but in the trick it is used as if it were the repeating decimal $\frac{1}{19}$.

As you would expect, the other nineteenths—$\frac{2}{19}$, $\frac{3}{19}$, $\frac{4}{19}$ and so on—are also repeating decimals, made up of the same digits.

$\frac{2}{19} =$ .105263157894736842. . . .
$\frac{3}{19} =$ .157894736842105263. . . .
$\frac{4}{19} =$ .210526315789473684. . . .

Compare these numbers with the products obtained when 2, 3, and 4 are multiplied by the dazzler. These products are:

×2=   1052631578947368420
×3=   15789473684201052630
×4=20105263157894736840

In each case, the digits are identical except for the zero at the end. This holds true through $\frac{18}{19}$. When the numerator in the fraction matches the multiplier, the digits in the decimal and the product are identical except for the final zero. That's why the trick works automatically.

Using the Binary System as a Code

Ordinarily we use the denary system of numbers, based on ten digits: 0, 1, 2, 3, 4, 5, 6, 7, 8. 9. The binary system, however, is based on only two digits: 0 and 1. Place-value notation is used in the system, so the value of each digit in a number depends on its position. Value increases by multiples of two. The place farthest to the right tells how many ones a number contains; the next, how many twos; then how many fours; how many eights, and so on.

Here are the numbers from zero through fifteen as they are written in binary notation:

0000=0	0100=4	1000=8	1100=12
0001=1	0101=5	1001=9	1101=13
0010=2	0110=6	1010=10	1110=14
0011=3	0111=7	1011=11	1111=15

The numbers from sixteen to thirty-one are written with five digits. A sixth digit at the left of the sixteens place would tell how many thirty-twos are in a number, since all the numbers from thirty-two to sixty-three are written with six digits. There is no limit to the size of a number than can be written in binary, but the largest one that appears in any of the tricks described here is sixty-three.

The binary system is easily adapted to codes. Any two different elements can be substituted for the digits 0 and 1, so numbers that don't look like numbers can be worked out and used in tricks.

Heads or Tails (page 28), a mind-reading trick, depends on a code in which the heads of coins stand for 0 and the tails stand for 1. By tossing three coins, you can produce any binary number from zero to seven.

Oriental Coin Toss (page 94), a fortunetelling trick, depends on using the binary system for a code. Since six coins are tossed, any binary number from zero to sixty-three can be produced.

I Ching patterns can be read as binary numbers because each is made by combining two different elements. In the pattern, the elements are unbroken and broken lines, which correspond to the symbols 0 and 1 of the binary system. The binary numbers from zero to eight, for example, correspond to these nine I Ching patterns:

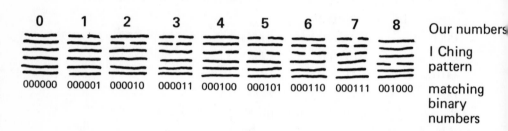

0	1	2	3	4	5	6	7	8	Our numbers
									I Ching pattern
000000	000001	000010	000011	000100	000101	000110	000111	001000	matching binary numbers

Who Did It? (page 79), a spooky trick, uses holes in cards as the 0 digit and slits as the digit for 1. Examine the cards with this in mind and you will see why the trick works.

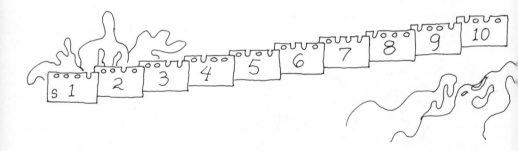

THE FUTURESCOPE (page 96), supposedly a fortunetelling machine, turns out to be a device for finding a chosen number. A spectator touches circles containing this number. The performer adds the top numbers of the circles touched, and this gives him the chosen number.

The Futurescope Circles

Notice that no two circles are alike. Each is marked with a different set of numbers, placed so that the smallest one is on top. Offhand, the numbers in a circle seem to have nothing in common. But you know that the trick wouldn't work unless they were related in some way. To understand their relationship, check the table of binary numbers (page 115). It provides the key to the trick.

When written in as four-digit binaries, the numbers in the circle with

1 on top have the digit 1 in the ones place. They include
0001, 0011, 0101, 0111, 1001, 1011, 1101, 1111

2 on top have the digit 1 in the twos place. They include
0010, 0011, 0110, 0111, 1010, 1011, 1110, 1111

4 on top have the digit 1 in the fours place. They include
0100, 0101, 0110, 0111, 1100, 1101, 1110, 1111

8 on top have the digit 1 in the eights place. They include
1000, 1001, 1010, 1011, 1100, 1101, 1110, 1111

With this arrangement, if all four circles are touched, it means a spectator's chosen number is 1111 in binary, the sum of 1+2+4+8, which equals 15. If only the circle with 8 on top is touched, then the spectator's chosen number is 1000 in binary, the sum of 8+0+0+0, which equals 8.

Intersecting Sets

Magic seems far removed from the math dealing with sets until you remember that a set is any collection of elements. Any group of cards—a hand, a row, a stack—can qualify as a set; any two groups with cards in common can be regarded as intersecting sets. For example, if each row and column in an array of cards is a separate set, then the card that is common to the top row and the first column is the intersection of two sets. This concept is useful in many tricks.

Nearly everyone is familiar with the method of locating an unknown card in an array of twelve or sixteen cards. After the spectator secretly picks a card, the performer locates it by asking which row and which column the card is in. In other words, the performer finds out where two sets of cards intersect.

Four at a Time (page 90) is based on the same principle, but it is disguised by dealing out the cards. You deal out five hands of five cards each, including a hand to yourself. The other four people each choose one of the cards they hold, and you are to identify the chosen cards.

Assume that the cards dealt out are the ones shown in the diagram below and those circled are the chosen cards:

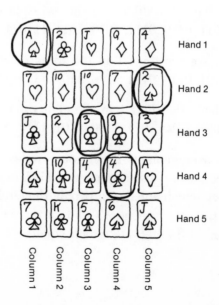

Now consider the cards in each hand and in each column as separate sets. Then the ace of spades is the intersection of Hand 1 and Column 1, and each of the other chosen cards are intersections of two sets.

To locate these cards, all are asked to put their hands on the table, face down. You do this too. Then you collect all the cards, stacking them so that Hand 1 is at the bottom, Hand 2 next, and so on, with your hand on top. Next you redeal the cards so that each person has a new set. The former holder of Hand 1 now has the set that was in Column 1, which is made up of everyone's former first card. Not only that, the cards are in the order in which people are seated. The holder of the second hand has everyone's second card—those formerly in Column 2—and they, too, are in the order in which people are seated. This is also true of the sets in the hands of the others.

Next the hands are laid down, one at a time. You ask the people to inspect each hand and tell you if their chosen card is in it. This information is all you need to locate the four chosen cards, because the first hand put down is the set that formed Column 1; the second hand, the set from Column 2, and so on. Consequently when someone says his chosen card shows up, his position indicates which card it is.

Algebra Provides the Answers

A magician never thinks of the terms x and y when performing. Yet quite a few number tricks are algebra problems that have been given magical masks.

CALENDAR CAPER (page 38) is a baffler until it is analyzed as an algebra problem. The performer takes the smallest number in a square of sixteen dates, multiplies it by 4, and adds 48 to get a predicted sum. If x equals that smallest number, then this is the formula for the trick:

$$4x+48=\text{the predicted sum}$$

To see why the formula works, take your square of sixteen numbers, the smallest of which is 1, and substitute algebraic values for them. When x=1, this is what you get:

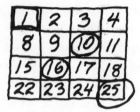 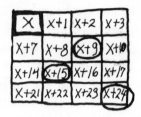

In the trick, four numbers—1, 10, 16, and 25—are not crossed out. Taking the sum of their algebraic values gives:

$$
\begin{array}{r}
x \\
x+\ 9 \\
x+15 \\
x+24 \\
\hline
4x+48
\end{array}
$$

And there's the secret formula for the trick.

The trick is set up so that each uncanceled number is in a different row as well as in a different column. This means that with x standing for the smallest number, the total of the four numbers will be at least $x+(x+7)+(x+14)+(x+21)$. How much more than that will it be? The value of the uncanceled number in the second column will be one more than any of those terms. The value of the number in the third column will be two more; that of the last number, three more. So the sum of the four uncanceled numbers comes to:

$$x+(x+7)+(x+14)+(x+21)+(1+2+3)=4x+48$$

What if different numbers are left in the square at the end of the trick? The sum of their algebraic values will be the same and the formula will work. It will work for any square of sixteen numbers, taken from any calendar page. The same algebraic values can be given to the numbers, since every week has seven days.

Tapping the Hours (page 42) involves two different counts: the spectator's and the magician's. Since the outcome in both cases is the same number, the trick can be explained by an equation. One side of this equation shows the results of the spectator's activities, expressed in mathematical terms, and the other side, the magician's results.

First, the magician's activities. The trick is set up so that he goes around the clock, tapping numbers at random and counting them until he reaches seven. Then he makes sure the eighth tap is on 12. After that, the magician moves backward, tapping one number at a time until the spectator calls stop. At this point he is on the spectator's secretly chosen number.

How in the world, you might ask, can that be stated mathematically? Well, start with the magician at the outset of the trick. He has no idea of how many taps will be required to get him to the chosen number. But he does know it will be more than eight. So if x equals the number of taps beyond eight, the total number of taps he makes will be $8+x$. The magician also knows the eighth tap will be on 12, and all those taps after it will be on smaller numbers. So the chosen number must equal $12-x$.

Now consider the spectator's activities. In counting the magician's taps, he starts with his chosen number and stops at 20. Then 20 minus his chosen number equals the number of taps.

To bring this all together, substitute $12-x$ for the chosen number. Now you have the whole equation:

$$20-(12-x)=8+x$$

And that's why the trick works. No wonder the old-time magicians had trouble explaining it!

HOUDINI, ARE YOU HERE? (page 72) conceals the problem involved through the use of cards. Forget the cards and treat the trick as a straight number problem. Look at it this way.

The number you get when you—	Substituting x for the number that is picked—
1) pick any number from 1 to 20	1) x
2) double that number	2) 2x
3) then add 8	3) 2x+8
4) divide the sum by 2	4) $\dfrac{2x+8}{2} = x+4$
5) subtract the original number from the result obtained	5) (x+4)−x=4

Since the x's cancel out, the result of these operations will always be 4. Naturally, when you do the trick, that's the answer you get from Houdini's ghost.

THE SEER'S CARD APPEARS (page 41) can be explained by letting x stand for the unknown number of cards that are added to the four on the table.

In step 1) the seer's card is at the bottom of a deck of *fifty-two* cards. Its position is 52.

In step 2) *twelve* cards are removed from the deck. Since 52−12=40, the seer's card is now in position 40. It remains there when four are left on the table.

In step 3) x cards are dealt from the deck and placed on these four. Now the seer's card is in position (40−x).

In step 4) 40−x cards are dealt from the deck. So the last one is the seer's card.

DOMINO DIVINATION (page 44) can be explained if you let x stand for the dots on one half of the chosen domino and y stand for the dots on the other half. Expressing each step in the trick in this way, you immediately see why the trick works, no matter which domino is chosen.

The computation steps	Expressed in algebra
1) Double the value of the dots on one half of the domino by 5	1) 5x
2) Add 7	2) 5x+7
3) Double the sum	3) 10x+14
4) Add the number of dots on the other half of the domino	4) 10x+14+y
5) Subtract 14, which gives the two-digit number sought by the performer	5) 10x+14−14+y=10x+y, which stands for the two-digit number telling how many dots are on each half of the domino

FATEFUL CHOICE (page 88) is the same problem, but this time the two unknowns are the value and suit of a card. If x equals the value and y the suit, the trick is easily explained.

Instructions to spectator	Algebra involved
1) Double the value of the card	1) 2x
2) Add 3	2) 2x+3
3) Multiply the sum by 5	3) 5(2x+3)
4) Depending on suit, add 1, 2, 3, or 4	4) 5(2x+3)+y or 10x+15+y
Performer's final step	
5) Subtract 15 from the total	5) 10x+15+y−15 gives 10x+y, the two-digit number the performer seeks

BEAT THE CALCULATOR (page 50) makes use of a short cut that works in adding ten numbers in the series set up in the trick. With x as the first number and y as the second number, the series total comes to 55x+88y. So, after the first two numbers are set up, you can get the final total if you multiply the first one by 55 and the second one by 88 and then add the two. In a show, this may be hard to do mentally if x and y have high values, but it is not so difficult for some lower values. If x=3 and y=2, then the total equals 165+176, or 341.

Two Against One (page 62) is truly confounding until it is analyzed algebraically. To see why the trick works, go through the operations using x for the audience's first number, y for the second, and xy for their product. Then, for the first number, you use 10,000−x; for the second number, y−1.

Multiply them and you get:

$$10,000-x$$
$$\times \quad y-1$$
$$\overline{-10,000+x}$$
$$10,000y \qquad\qquad -xy$$
$$\overline{10,000y-10,000+x-xy}$$

This product can be regrouped and written:

$$10,000(y-1)+x-xy$$

Then, adding the product of the audience's two numbers, xy, eliminates the term xy. The sum you get is:

$$10,000(y-1)+x$$

The key to the trick is the expression 10,000 (y−1). Substitute the number used in the stage directions, 7845, for it and multiply by 10,000; then you get:

$$7845$$
$$\times 10,000$$
$$\overline{78,450,000}$$

Then adding 5329, the number x stands for $+ \quad 5329$

gives: $\overline{78,455,329}$

Place-value Notation

In our system of writing numbers of two or more digits, the position of each digit determines its value. The first digit tells how many tens the number contains; the second tells how many ones. For example, 12 means 1 ten plus 2 ones; 21 means 2 tens plus 1 one. Since the place value of the digits increases by multiples of ten, in any three-digit number the first digit tells how many hundreds are in the number; in a four-digit number, it tells how many thousands are in the number, and so on.

By using letters in place of digits, any number of more than one digit can be expressed according to this scheme:

10b+1a — a two-digit number

100c+10b+1a — a three-digit number

1000d+100c+10b+1a — a four-digit number

These expressions, as you will see, come in handy when you try to explain tricks and puzzles involving place value.

Egg Eggstraordinary (page 45) starts with a two-digit number. Let 10b+1a stand for this number. Adding its two digits, as in the trick, gives: b+a. Then subtracting this sum from the number gives:

$$10b+1a$$
$$-\quad b-1a$$
$$\overline{9b}$$

Since a can be any digit, the value of 9a is $9{\times}a$ and may be shown by the 9 times table:

$$9{\times}2=18$$
$$9{\times}3=27$$
$$9{\times}4=36$$

and so on.

Notice that each product is a number with two digits that add up to 9. So the final number in the trick is always 9.

Haunted Cards (page 70) can be explained in the same way. When you do the trick,

In step 1) the count of the cards in the packet comes to: $\quad 10b+1a$

In step 2) the sum of the two digits gives: $\quad 1b+1a$

In step 3) taking that number of cards from the packet is like subtracting them and gives:

$$10b+1a$$
$$-\quad 1b-1a$$
$$\overline{9b}$$

Since the number of cards in the packet is from 20 to 29, the first digit in the number is 2. Substitute 2 for b, and there's the crucial number in the trick: 18.

TELEPHONEY (page 25) involves a three-digit number beginning and ending with different digits. A second number is formed by reversing the digits. If the smaller number is subtracted from the larger, the result is divisible by 99. To see why, write the terms algebraically, then subtract them:

$$100c+10b+1a$$
$$1c-10b-100a$$
$$\overline{99c \qquad - \quad 99a}$$

SPIRIT WRITING (page 76) also involves a three-digit number that can be expressed as $100c+10b+1a$. Dividing this by the sum of its digits gives:

$$\frac{100c+10b+1a}{1c+ \ 1b+1a}$$

Since the three digits of the number in the trick are the same, a can be substituted for b, and for c. Then the expression can be rewritten this way:

$$\frac{100a+10a+1a}{1a+ \ 1a+1a}$$

Adding the a's gives:

$$\frac{111a}{3a}, \text{ which equals } 37$$

As you see, it doesn't matter what digit a stands for. In doing the trick, the outcome will always be 37.

THE TABLE TAPS THE ANSWER (page 73) is tricky. Instead of using $1000d+100c+10b+1a$ for the four-digit number, substitute $(999+1)d+(99+1)c+(9+1)b+1a$ and divide by 9. This gives:

$$\frac{999d}{9}+\frac{99c}{9}+\frac{9b}{9}+\frac{1a+1d+1c+1b}{9} \text{ or}$$

$$\frac{111d+11c+1b+1a+1b+1c+1d}{9}$$

Those first three terms stand for whole numbers, no matter what a, b, and c equal. But the fourth term, $\dfrac{1a+1b+1c+1d}{9}$, equals a whole number only if the sum of all four digits—a, b, c, d—is divisible by nine. If you analyze numbers of fewer or more digits in the same way, you see that the rule holds for all of them: a number is divisible by nine only when the sum of its digits is divisible by nine.

THE SPOOK TAKES A HAND (page 78) is a multiplication problem—the squaring of a two-digit number ending in five. Let's say the number is 35. Representing it algebraically as 10a+5, the steps go like this:

in arithmetic	*in algebra*
step 1) the first digit is multiplied by the next higher one: $3 \times 4 = 12$	$3 \times (3+1)$ or $a(a+1)$
step 2) using the product for the first two digits is equivalent to	$12 \times (100)$ or $100a(a+1)$
step 3) square the second digit, 5	$5 \times 5 = 25$
step 4) writing the total is the equivalent of adding steps 2 and 3, giving 1225	$1200+25$, or $100a(a+1) = 25$

Now $100a(a+1)+25$ equals $100a^2+100a+25$. As you see, this is the product obtained when $10a+5$ is squared:

$$
\begin{array}{r}
10a + 5 \\
\times\ 10a + 5 \\
\hline
100a^2 + 50a \\
50a+25 \\
\hline
100a^2+100a+25
\end{array}
$$

And that's why the trick works.

INDEX